ENLIST

Veteran's Histories

D0651025

Melvin F. Cruthers

Note for Librarians: A cataloguing record for this book is available from Library and Archives
Canada at www.collectionscanada.ca/amicus/index-e.html
ISBN 1-4120-6138-5

*Printed in Victoria, BC, Canada. Printed on paper with minimum 30% recycled fibre. Trafford's print shop
runs on "green energy" from solar, wind and other environmentally-friendly power sources.*

Offices in Canada, USA, Ireland and UK
This book was published *on-demand* in cooperation with Trafford Publishing. On-demand
publishing is a unique process and service of making a book available for retail sale to the
public taking advantage of on-demand manufacturing and Internet marketing. On-demand
publishing includes promotions, retail sales, manufacturing, order fulfilment, accounting and
collecting royalties on behalf of the author.

Book sales for North America and international:
Trafford Publishing, 6E–2333 Government St.,
Victoria, BC v8t 4p4 CANADA
phone 250 383 6864 (toll-free 1 888 232 4444)
fax 250 383 6804; email to orders@trafford.com
Book sales in Europe:
Trafford Publishing (uk) Ltd., Enterprise House, Wistaston Road Business Centre,
Wistaston Road, Crewe, Cheshire cw2 7rp UNITED KINGDOM
phone 01270 251 396 (local rate 0845 230 9601)
facsimile 01270 254 983; orders.uk@trafford.com
Order online at:
trafford.com/05-1039

10 9 8 7 6 5 4 3 2 1

ACKNOWLEDGEMENT

I wish to acknowledge
Major Jason E. Seyer
For his graduation picture
From Cardinal High School,
Middlefield, Ohio in 1990.
Went from High School
To Ohio Northern University
And joined ROTC at
Bowling Green, Ohio.
Joined the United States
Air Force where he has
Enjoyed considerable travel.
His Grandfather, Emanuel
Magilavy is in this book,
Also of the United States
Air Force.

FORWARD

My intent in writing this book is to try and get a message across to members of High School graduates to consider enlisting in the services of the United States. At this time in history it is almost impossible for the average family to send their sons and daughters to college at the current escalating costs. A four year stint in the service of their choice will make them eligible to attend a college of their choice with the aid of the government. This book will relate the stories of many current and ex-service personnel and their attitudes toward the time that they spent in the services. It was a time of adventure, growth, maturity, travel, discipline and life long comradery. Not one regretted their time spent in the service even under adverse conditions. Many regretted leaving instead of making it a career. Others who experienced war time conditions said that they wouldn't ever want to go through that again but wouldn't take a million dollars for the experience. Basically they all highly recommended High School graduates to consider the military experience. In fact, particularly WWII Veterans suggests that a bus be backed up to the High School door and load all able graduates to the nearest recruiting station. All Veterans don't harbor that thought.

I hope you enjoy the histories here-in and in some way help to get the message across that it is not a bad thing for graduates to consider.

JAMES A. BAUMGARTNER

James A. Baumgartner, 14680 Rapids Road, Burton, Ohio 44021

Born January 13, 1948 in Russell, Ohio and raised at 8955 Fairmount Road, Novelty, Ohio, Russell Township.

He graduated from West Geauga High School in 1966.

In October of 1997 he felt he was going to be drafted so he went up to the draft board to check his status and he was told that his number was coming up in November. He waited for the short period and was drafted in the middle of November. This was a two year active duty stint.

He went to boot camp at Fort Knox, Kentucky and they had eight weeks of boot camp, which was actually nine weeks because they had what they called a zero week. That week was spent in indoctrination, getting shots, outfitting, hair cuts and assigning units. In the middle of his boot camp, which was about the middle of December, they sent them home. This was something Very unusual during boot camp but just because the D.I.'s and everybody in Fort Knox didn't want to be around over the Christmas Holiday. They wanted Christmas to so they shut down the boot camp until after the Holiday. He had two weeks leave.

When he got back he went through some more training and it got to be an unusual cold spell going on down there. He said that the Army had a regulation that if it got to be ten degrees or below they didn't want you to do any training outside. So they did indoor training and exercises. The cold spell lasted for about two weeks so they had a very easy boot camp experience. When they did get some decent weather they went to the rifle range and he got the citation for the best marksman in his unit. He knocked his target down ninety nine percent of the time at three hundred yards with a M-14 rifle. It's a very accurate rifle and it is also used as a sniper rifle. He got a unit citation and a trophy with it.

They shipped him to Fort Gordon, Georgia. After Boot Camp they give tests to see where you are best suited and he guessed that they decided that he was best suited for the Signal Corp. He spent two months there for Signal Corp training. The atmosphere was quite relaxed at Fort Gordon and when you weren't on duty at night you could go off base and visit friends, live off base, if you could afford it, or visit some of your married buddies that had quarters off base. During the day he had his training. At the end of his training they called all of them in formation and they would call out names telling them who was going to go where. Some were going to go to Germany, some to Korea and those that were chosen to go to Germany or Korea instead of Vietnam all had long faces. They didn't want to go to those locations, they hoped to be going to Vietnam. When he and the others were chosen to go to Vietnam they all stood up and cheered. He was glad to find himself going into a war zone. This was for a one year tour of duty in Vietnam.

He had another two week leave, but that was the last one he got for over a year, he then went to Australia for R and R and then he was out of the service.

After the two week leave they went to Fort Lewis, Washington getting all the stuff they would need to go to Vietnam. They were issued no weapons but their shots and everything they needed to go overseas. They spent two or three days there and then they put them on a plane. They stopped off at Hawaii to refuel then to Guam for more refueling, just like island hopping. They were on a DC-10 which could take over three hundred passengers. It was a civilian aircraft. It was a fourteen hour trip with Stewardess and all. It was interesting to look at all the islands as they passed over Hawaii and Guam looked really tiny and it was interesting to see all the B-52's lined up along the runway. From Guam they went to Vietnam to Cam Ranh Bay. When they got off the plane it was so hot and humid over there that they could hardly breath. Especially after flying in the air conditioned plane. They shipped them to a temporary barracks and the next day they set them up in bleachers to listen to a guy talk explaining what to expect, what to look for and all of a sudden here came someone out of the ground shooting blanks at them. It scared the dickens out of them. What they were doing is simulating what the enemy would do and how they would camouflage themselves by hiding in the ground. They were informed that this is what you can expect when you are here. That really woke them up. Then they told them that they were going to outfit them with M-16's.

They had never fired them before and didn't know what they looked like. They had been trained with the M-14. They were taken to a firing range to become familiar with the M-16. The M-16 was a lot different, they were a lot lighter, smaller and not as accurate as the M-14 especially at long range. They are an assault rifle and you can use them automatic or semi-automatic, and he said that they were actually a nice little weapon and you can carry them around easily and they even had a handle on them.

They were all transients and they were to be shipped to where ever they were needed. He went to An Khe temporarily until they decided where they were going to keep him. Then they sent him to Camp Evans which was about thirty miles from the DMZ. That's where the First Cavalry Division was. He was with the First Cavalry Thirteenth Signal Corp. His job was to install telephone communication from a trailer that they pulled with a Jeep. The trailer was nothing but telephone communication equipment and they would run land lines from that to any landing zone (LZ) command bunker. Whoever the officers were that used the phones would send messages back to the trailer and they would shoot it via antenna to the next receiver but not more than twenty or thirty miles distant. That was the extent of there range. They could shoot it to another landing zone or a rear base. There were a lot of landing zones in Vietnam so they were always within range. Also receiving return messages to forward back to the landing zone command bunker. The longest he stayed on any landing zone was about two months. Normally he stayed a month or five weeks. Then he would be moved to another landing zone. If he wasn't supporting an artillery group he would be supporting infantry. Any landing zone he was attached to there would be some artillery as well as a group of infantry. The artillery would give fire support to the infantry when they moved out, firing in advance of their movements. He never had to move with the troops in the jungle even though he was stationed near the jungle only in a protected area behind barbed wire in bunkers. He lived like that for a whole year over there.

Right after he arrived at Camp Evans the Sergeant approached him and wanted to know if he objected to being with any blacks. He said that he certainly wasn't prejudiced. So then he sent him and two colored troops up to this mountain top near Hue that had just gotten overrun the night before and he didn't know that until he got there. There was only a few of them that went up there and they had to set up a few signal units to get them communicated. He was only there for a day and a night. It was a barren hilltop with everything blown up. One of the reasons they needed him to go up there was that one of his signal men called 'Tiny' who was about six foot three and two hundred thirty pounds had just been killed. He was sent there for temporary replacement.

One time they had an incoming round that came in, it was a mortar that blew up a jeep not to far from their bunker, about fifty to seventy five feet away. The shrapnel from the round cut the guide lines to the antenna. When something like this happens the unit sends off a sound like a blaring tone to tell you something isn't right. It woke them up and they were trying to get the system to work with no success until they decided to look outside and discovered the antenna on the ground. There is three of them on a team and sometimes they are the only Americans on a landing zone, the rest of them are all ARVN Troops, Army Republic of Vietnam or South Vietnam Troops. They had to attach new guide lines to get the antenna back up and reset the phones to get them working again. The bunkers were built well enough that a mortar round wouldn't get through to them but it wiped out the jeep.

The Americans got along excellent with the ARVN Troops. One of the members of the ARVN Troops by the name of Lt. Kwan, as he remembers, he got along good with. They had camouflage suits that he really liked so he asked if he could get one to take home with him. Actually they were too small for him to wear but he was so impressed with them that he wanted one to take home. He ended up getting two pair of them. He asked for the biggest they had but even then they were too small, because the Vietnamese were small people. They would cook for them once in a while and they processed their own rice and would cook rice for them. He said that the way they cooked it wasn't like anything he ever found stateside. It was rice straight out of the field and it was excellent. They use to prepare holiday meals and include them and they were excellent cooks.

He actually got an early out, in those days the Marines and the Army were offered an early out but you had to qualify for it. He was there for twelve months and his Master Sergeant told him that he could get an early out but he would have to qualify for it. The Sergeant said that he would have to stay one more month to qualify for it, or go home, take a thirty day leave, come back if you want or spend the rest of your time stateside. They only did this for men in the war zone. He stayed for the thirteenth month. He went home and his tour of duty was over except that he was in the active reserves for two years and the inactive reserves for another two years.

He said that basically he had it pretty easy. There were a couple of times when he was on these landing zones that they got hit during the night. They were informed that there was a good chance that they would be over run by the enemy. There were only about thirty troops at this landing zone and that particular night they were all on guard duty. He called in a "Spooky Gun Ship", back then they had WWII airplanes, two engine prop jobs, C-47's that they called Spooky. They were mounted with mini guns that as he recalls would fire about 35 hundred rounds a minute. They had several of them on these gun ships and every fifth round was a tracer. It was at night time and when they shot off their weapons out of the sky it looked like one giant whip, one solid red line. The commanding officer said that any one that wanted to shoot out front into the jungle – have at it! They used grenade launchers and they had a lot of ammunition so they just shot wildly into the jungle. Tanks were brought in to reinforce there position. After that they had no more problems. Later they sent out recon troops to see if any thing happened and they came upon a few dead bodies but no one knew who got them. That was the scariest time he had but they were always getting mortar rounds into their bases but more for harassment then any thing else. Some times in the day time and some times at night. They would usually fire several rounds but when you seen where the first two rounds landed you could usually tell where the proceeding rounds would land. They did have a rear base tent blow up on them once when an incoming round came in and a good buddy of his got killed. Jim Berends lived by the Chesapeake Bay in Maryland and they went to boot camp together and AIT together. Jim Berends was stationed in the rear and they got a call that he was killed. They couldn't believe it because the rear bases were considered the safest. He had just been back there recently and in the tent that got hit. If he had been there he could have probably been killed also. The round landed next to Berends bunk killing him and wounding several others. When you were stationed in a landing zone you were on your own. No one brought you anything, except a good supply of C-Rations, so you had to make trips back to pick up food, drinks and supplies unless you can get it off the ARVN Troops. Once in a while you can hitch a ride on a helicopter going to one of your rear bases. Sometimes you get stuck at the rear base before you can return. One other time he and a buddy made a beer and a pop run to a Marine base about ten miles near the DMZ. They got about ten cases of each and when they made a run like this they wore their flak jackets, helmets and took their weapons to fight in case you had to. When they got back the Sergeant said, "Didn't you know that was a red alert zone you drove through?" He said there was no way of knowing this after they were on the road and at the Marine base no one said anything because they were

Army and he didn't think the Marines gave a dam. They could have been ambushed but they didn't know that.

He has been at the Vietnam Memorial in Washington and has visited the traveling Memorial and looked up his friend Jim Berends name and scratched it off with a pencil on a piece of paper. They had discussed his visiting him at his home and going deep sea fishing in the Chesapeake Bay. His father had his own fishing boat and took out fishing charters. They had all got together and sent money, flowers and letters to his parents in sympathy.

He got to Vietnam in May of 1968 and got out in June of 1969. Coming back they took a different route flying over to Japan at an Army Base where they stayed over night and were fed. Then they were flown into San Francisco and took the buss over the Oakland Bay Bridge to Oakland. They were transferred out of the service in Oakland. He then flew home.

When he got home he served active and inactive reserve without ever having been called to attend any meetings or encampments. He never understood why he and some of his other friends had never been called to reserve duties. He thought that maybe it was because they had served in war zones and felt they had already seen enough service.

He received his Army discharge while in Oakland on June 16, 1969

His rating was E-4 (Specialist 4) when discharged.

His medals are National Defense Service Medal, Vietnam Service Medal, Vietnam Campaign Medal and rifle marksman medal.

He got married June 22nd 1974 to Doris Campbell. He has five step children and two children of his own with Doris.

He didn't take advantage of the G.I. Bill but took advantage of machine shop jobs to learn enough to start his own business. He operates his own business under the name of "Machine Magic" located in Middlefield, Ohio on Nauvoo Road.

JAMES R. BAUMGARTNER

James R. Baumgartner, 8915 Fairmount Road, Novelty, Ohio 44072

Born April 18, 1926, Fairmount Road, Novelty, Ohio

High School in Russell Township, graduated in 1943

He enlisted in the U. S. Marine Corp in Cleveland, Ohio October 26th, 1943.

He went to boot Camp in San Diego, California and rifle range at Camp Matthews then basic training at Camp Elliot. He shipped out on March 5th, 1944 and was sent to Hawaii where he became attached to the 5th Amphibious Corp. His job was to unload and load ships, mostly ammunition that they would move to an ammunition dump. Between ships he said they would play soldier and they thought that they were getting ready to move out to the front. They were just keeping us busy and in shape until the next ship. He said that when he had to perform the exercise of crawling under barbed wire while machine guns were firing over them it use to scare the hell out of him. They would tell them to keep their heads and butts down and he surely did. At Camp Elliot it was only basic training and any duties in the Amphibious Corp. was held in Hawaii. He got in Oahu and they threw them off in a lumber yard and had them moving lumber from one side of the road to the other. They didn't tell them about the sun and he received one of the worst sun burns he's ever had.

Then they sent them to another island and they stayed there over a year. They unloaded ships while others were firing at targets. He was on Kauai all of 1944. While there he learned to operate fork lifts and cranes. In 1945 they moved to the big island of Hawaii where they loaded up for Japan. They were there for two or three months while they gathered up people and loaded up ships to go to Japan. They went to Japan as part of the occupation forces. They got there after the surrender papers were signed. They moved out in a huge convoy and they moved with all lights out and zig zagging as they moved. When they got about half way they quit zig zagging and they could have lights on. They got all concerned that there might be a submarine out there that didn't get the word that the war was over. They landed in Japan and stayed there for quite a while until he built up enough points to be sent home. They left Japan in the first part of January, 1946. While in Japan he hitched a ride and saw the second city that was hit by the atom bomb, Hiroshima. Sasebo was the city as close as they could get and they could see it from a distance. In Japan they were still loading and unloading ships. They were given some colored troops and some Japanese to do the work and they were acting as bosses to get the work done. This was in Sasebo on the island of Kyushu. When they got there they were greeted by many children and the little girls would be carrying the boys, the little children on their shoulders. They would never see any young men. The city was in very bad shape from all the bombing, the sewers were bad and sidewalks broken. They never experienced any of the shelling or bombings but they were there all the time. They used all old Japanese men who could put heavy loads on their shoulders, two would lift up the load and place it on the shoulders of the third man and he would walk away with it. In the evening the cooks would bring them their meals and they would set around a camp fire with the Japanese and sometime they would make remarks to them that weren't very complimentary and the Japanese wouldn't understand. Sometimes they would just smile and bow and others would look upset because they didn't understand. Basically they got along with them very well. The Japanese would do anything you'd want.

When they landed in Japan they all carried their M-1 rifles but they weren't issued any ammunition. It was a little scary but fortunately they didn't need them. He said that in the evening and night they would see some pretty large men wandering the streets, larger than the normal Japanese, and then before daylight they would be gone.

They came back to the states on LST's they had ordered a bunch of trucks and they had a bunch of colored servicemen who he figured were truck drivers and it took thirty days to land in San Diego. The ramp came down and they unloaded the Jeeps and drove them up on the bank. Bulldozers pushed sand up to the ship to make a ramp. All day they unloaded the ship and then went back on board for the night. The Sailors were going to shore for liberty and he knew one of them so he asked him to call his sister who lived there. Pretty soon they called his name over the intercom and told him that he could go ashore because someone wanted to see him. It was his sister and friends. They had been going in and out of that ramp all afternoon and when he stepped off the ramp he landed in water up to his waist. The tide had come in and where the ship was anchored the tide had caused a watery drop after the ramp.

He got out of the service April 2nd, 1946. When they got home they got a thirty day leave, thirty days to get home and another thirty days to get all the way back to California to get discharged. He was discharged at Alameda, California. When he got to Alameda he had about two weeks to kill so they put an arm band on him like a MP with no training and placed him in an intersection. They had civilians working there that left and entered and they told him to direct traffic and if an officer or a General came up let them right through. He said that he didn't know a Generals car from any other but he guessed he got lucky because everything went alright. He spent about three weeks with the armband until his discharge.

He said that actually he was very well cared for because he never got into any action except when someone came in drunk and slipped in the shower room and got hurt. One drunk come out of this little town and fell out of the truck and got squished by the dual wheels. That was his only casualty.

Medals earned were Good Conduct Medal, Asiatic-Pacific Campaign Medal, American Campaign Medal and World War 11 Victory Medal

He married Theresa Talarcek May 1st, 1947. They have four children, James Allen, Janet, Vicki and Jack.

His best buddy in the Marine Corp was Jim Anger, Michigan.

He worked for the Village of Hunting Valley in the service department and retired February 1st, 1987.

JOHN RICHARD BENDOKAITIS,JR.

John R. Bendokaitis, 17182 Eastview Drive, Chagrin Falls, Ohio 44023

He was born October 20, 1928 in Grand Rapids, Michigan.

He went to Union High School in Grand Rapids graduating in 1946. Then he went to the Grand Rapids Junior College graduating two years later then in 1948 he went to Michigan State majoring in mechanical engineering until entering the service.

After High School he was drafted in 1948 but due to the end of the war and the transferring of troops from Europe to Japan for occupational duty he was deferred. So he went to Michigan State taking mechanical engineering. While going to college he held a job the company felt critical during the Korean war. They attempted to have him deferred but the services finally decided he was needed. He was inducted into the Army at Fort Wayne in Detroit, Michigan on March 29, 1951. He was sent to Fort Custer for processing and than combined with others from Michigan who were shipped by train to Fort Sill. He and most of the others were assigned to a Reserve unit out of Salt Lake City, Utah. After boot camp his advanced training in artillery observation was all held in Oklahoma. In fact, except for a period when they went on maneuvers in Texas, his whole tour of duty was in Oklahoma.

When he went into the services he was combined with two outfits who were becoming POR (Prepare Overseas Replacements) qualified. It was like a contest to become POR qualified. They were in training and then one of the outfits went overseas and the other one stayed and became a replacement training outfit, which included John. He was assigned to the 653rd Field Artillery Observation Battalion. It was a specialty battalion. They had sight, sound and radar detection systems which was support for the artillery. It turned out to be support for the Atomic Cannon. The 280mm Atomic Cannon was a hush-hush system being developed and tested at Fort Sill. They had exercises to sight in the Atomic Cannon, interpreting the trajectory of the cannon with field exercises, etc. It was a 280mm inch naval gun. The Atomic Cannon fired a 280mm inch shell and they would fire them at Ft Sill without the atomic war head to justify the computer calculations. They would back the gun up against the East Range fence and fire it into the Wichita Mountains a distance of thirty five miles, on a low charge. Normally it would carry fifty miles, minimum. When firing they would take officers in training out to the range to sight in where shells landed. They also did exercises in all other artillery such as the 155's, 105's, 75's, etc. Fort Sill was a training center for new officers and John's group was setting up classes for these new Officers, to be, taking them out on field exercises, classes in Trigonometry, survey, radar and radar equipment, sight and sound.

They went on maneuvers down in Ft. Hood, Texas, Operation Longhorn, which was the exercises and training for going to Korea. John with a couple of officers and a radio operator were umpires for Operation Longhorn. They stayed out in the middle of the range observing the operation. Artillery pieces were assigned targets and it was the umpires job to check the ability of the gunners to properly set up, fire and hit assigned targets.

John was married just before this maneuver and since he was a draftsman he volunteered and became an assistant in operations, doing maps and reports, etc. The Commanding Officer from battalion headquarters said that if he went home and got married that he would make sure that he didn't go overseas. So he got married and his bride moved down outside of Fort Hood. He married Joan Swarts on December 29, 1951. Joining John while in the service, he said that they had a 'blast'. They joined a group of about a half a dozen others with common interests.

He almost became an officer because he had all the papers filled out and he had been in ROTC in high school and college, but he had been drafted out of college and didn't have his two years in ROTC. They encouraged him to become an officer but when he heard that he would have to sign up for seven years he said 'forget that.'

John was separated from the service march 28, 1953 and transferred to the U. S. Army Reserves. He received an honorable discharge with the rank of Corporal.

Upon discharge he used the G.I. Bill to take a course in Commercial Art and a course in Industrial Time Management. He credited the services after his discharge for his ability in management and teaching that he carried over into his civilian life. He credited his college education before he went into the service for some of the positions that he held while in the service and with some of his expanded duties he learned in the service for his success in civilian life.

John and his wife were blessed with five children. His oldest son went from high school into the U.S. Air Force. While in the Air Force he took advantage of College courses and the GI Bill for college, after the four years service, that have prepared him for his current position of Vice President of a big soft ware company in Scotsdale, Arizona.

John said that they wanted him to stay in the service because they were doing a lot of research in atomic weaponry. Seeing that he was now married and had served his time he elected to leave. He still belongs to an Army Reunion club and has a lot of respect for the services and what they have to offer and is of the mind, as many do, that every kid should serve a year or two in the service.

ARNOLD H. BOTTGER

Arnold H. Bottger, 10419 Cedar Road, Chesterland, Ohio 44026

Born April 27, 1922 in Newbury, Ohio.

Graduated from Newbury High School in 1941.

He was drafted into the Army December 16, 1942.

He entered active service December 23 1942 through Ft. Hayes, Ohio and was sent to Aberdeen Proving Grounds, Maryland for boot training. The rifle range was located right on the Chesapeake Bay and his basic training in Ordinance was also held right there.

He had his basic training in Aberdeen Maryland one day orders came for him to report to Fort Knox and being a green rookie he approached his Second Lieutenant and asked why he was being sent to Fort Knox. He said "Do you know what is at Fort Knox?" He said yes tanks and armor. He said there isn't much room in those tanks and you little fellows fit much better. He said, "I'm getting the picture." So he ended up in Knox. He ended up in the ordinance outfit. Two of them were sent to Santa Anita, California to a special small arms school. Hand and shoulder weapons repair schooling. They were told that by the time they were done they would be able to take the parts of any hand and shoulder weapon in the Armies arsenal that were thrown into a container and sort out the particular parts for any weapon they wished to assemble. They were right and when you assembled the particular weapon you chose you stepped up to a line and took the appropriate ammunition and test fired it. The training took seven weeks. Then back to Fort Knox.

One weekend a buddy and he went into Louisville on a weekend pass. He got sick with an attack of kidney stone. He wound up in Naples General Hospital in Louisville. One day he was lying in bed when in walked two armed guards, walked up to his bed and one of them said "Get dressed." He said that his clothes were in a closet and the one Guard said that "This man will get your clothes for you." He tried to ask what was going on, was he under arrest or what? He said that he hadn't done anything. The Guard said just do as we tell you. They had an ambulance backed up tight to the door. They escorted him down the hall, one on each side, he was still weak. They placed him in the ambulance and laid him down then asked him if he was comfortable. He said that he was comfortable enough but would sure as hell like to know what was going on. The Guard said that he would find out soon enough. He asked where they were going and the Guard replied that he couldn't tell him that. He raised up as he was going through a main gate and realized he was back at Fort Knox. They took him straight to the base hospital. As they backed up to the door the Guard said that if he met anybody in the hallway that you know you are not allowed to speak to them. He asked once again if he was under arrest or what. The Guard said no your not but that is all I can tell you. They put him to bed and before they left they said that at five o'clock there will be a Colonel in to explain some things to you. At five o'clock sharp this Colonel walked in and he said I guess you are wondering what the hell is going on. He said as a matter of fact I sure am. He said 'well you are one of several being picked to participate in a top secret project.' He asked if his unit was still here and the Colonel responded 'no'. He asked 'where are they?' The Colonel said that he couldn't tell him that but when he was well enough to leave the hospital he would join them. After a few days went by he was well enough and he was escorted by armed guard to the railroad station on base and every where the train stopped he would look out the window and there were armed guards standing so he wouldn't be able to talk to anybody on the platform. They brought all his meals to him in the compartment, they gave him no chance to converse with anybody. In the middle of the night after some three days the train stopped and he heard some of his buddies. He was away out in the middle of the desert. The rail head was Bouse, Arizona and they loaded him up on a truck and went to a camp built out in the middle of the desert where this special project was being conducted. This project was a dream of the British and they claimed that they didn't have the money or whatever to do it. That secret project was in anticipation of a great deal of resistance crossing the Cologne plain in Germany so they gave up this idea of making a four inch slit in the turret of the tank in which there was mounted a thirty five millimeter motion picture projector. In our training out there it worked. They did all their training at night and if you attempted to attack the tank it would go on and off and totally disorient them. These outfitted tanks operated behind the fighter tanks and the lights were so bright they would hide the muzzle blast of the fighter tanks. Even though he was in an ordinance outfit up there they trained like infantry. They had to dig fox holes and the tanks ran over the top of them. Every other weekend they got a pass to go to Phoenix and it was always twenty one and an officer. Never separated. They were called the hush-hush boys. Before they loaded the tanks to take them over they built canopies over the turrets so the slit wouldn't be exposed. They over did it. About thirty years or so there was a complete story in a newspaper about this top secret project which turned out to be a complete dud. The Germans were retreating so fast across the Cologne Plain by this time that they couldn't catch them.

They disembarked from New York on March 31, 1944 on the Queen Elizabeth. They were supposed to land in England but they were warned that an alert had sounded that the German air force was looking for them. So they dropped anchor in the Atlantic before they got to England and were transferred into smaller vessels to be taken on to England. They arrived April 8, 1944 close to Scotland and were transferred into trains and taken into Wales. That was where they finished their training. When they first went over they were attached to what they called the 9th army group, although they were the 5th armored division under the command of Montgomery. They went over the channel D plus 6. The Normandy beach and when they walked off the beach into the closest town they looked up and the first thing they saw was a Coca Cola sign. The silly things you remember. Every thing was secure by this time but it was still a helluva mess. His actions carried him all over France, Belgium, Luxemburg, Holland and Germany. It seemed that they just sent them where ever they needed them. His being a small arms repairman and Jeep driver for his Captain isolated him from a lot of the front line actions.

They were all traveling East and Patton was to their South, the British 2nd was to the North and the Canadian 1st was to the further North. When Patton was making his big drives, he sent his guys to hi-jack their fuel trucks. He was going to far, to fast and running out of fuel. Patton was going to fast and Eisenhower called him into

England seven different times and chewed him out but it didn't do any good. Patton had his own way of doing things.

When the war ended in Europe they found out about some very modern shower facilities in Germany, so they were looking forward to that. They loaded us on a truck and they took us there and the Captains driver, Tim, was carrying a Thompson Sub Machine Gun and he jumped off the back of the truck and the gun slammed on the sidewalk which caused it to discharge and the bullet went up through his chin and out the top of his head. The rest of them were already off the trucks and going into the building when they heard the shot. They looked around and seen Tim huddled upon the ground. It kind of took the pleasure out of the Shower. Because of this Arnie became the Captains driver. After several surgical procedures in France they flew Tim back to the states for more surgery.

Some years later Arnie and his wife, like a nightmare, they were walking down the aisle of the Palace Theatre in Cleveland when this hand reached out and grabbed him and it was Tim. They hugged each other bawling and the only effect it left him was he was wearing glasses. It was like a ghost reaching out.

After the war ended they pulled back into an assembly area in France and sat there for three days and nobody knew why. One day his Captain said to take him to

Army Headquarters. He went up some steps and there was an armed guard on each side and he gave them an elbow and in he went. He was sitting in the jeep out in the street and he could hear his Captain yelling at the General inside. After about twenty minutes he came out and for about two miles down the road the silence was deafening when he said 'well by God were not going to the South Pacific'. That's what they wanted because orders had come through to prepare our equipment for overseas shipment and they didn't mean back to the states. He said 'by God I told him'. He had a stack of citations and commendations that he laid down in front of the General and asked 'don't they have troops trained in the states that can go to the South Pacific'. So they sent them down into Austria where all they did was eat and sleep. They were supposed to guard a contingent of Hungarian prisoners of war. The Captain wanted to know if any one in the outfit spoke Hungarian. He did speak Hungarian so he was made the Captains interpreter. Then they found out that near where they were the Lipizzaner Stallions were hid out because they were afraid the Russians would find them. They had the privilege of going to the farm and sitting on these horses and had pictures taken. Some years later he heard that Tom Meyer, of the Meyers snow plow company, had been given the honor and privilege of buying one of these Lipizzaner Stallions. He heard that he was going to be at the Geauga County Fair so he took a copy of his photo on one of the horses and showed it to him. Mr Meyer's went berserk so he told him the story.

Captain Marshall Keith White, a heart of gold.

They captured a German Field Marshall, he was in a building but not exactly a hospital, but he wasn't well. He asked if he could be alone for twenty minutes and the only reason was to get into his full uniform and come down and surrender. That was the only way he felt honorable. Arnie said that we didn't out fight the Germans – we out equipped them. How could a bunch of country bumpkins out fight professionals such as the Germans who were trained in the military from the time they were twelve years old.

Once they were in Luxemburg and were bogged knee deep in mud. They were at the base of a mountain in pup tents with water running through them. One morning he had just come off guard duty off of the top of the mountain because they said that the Germans had just dropped paratroopers and everyone was a little nervous. In the morning some one yelled that the mess truck had just caught up to us. Arnie asked what they had and they answered powdered eggs. He just happened to really like powdered eggs so he sloshed down there in the mud with his mess gear. He looked over the side of the truck and there were large hunks of onions sticking up out of the eggs. He couldn't stand onions and he got so mad he threw his mess gear at the Mess Sergeant. The Sergeant said ,'hey I could court martial you for that'. Arnie said 'Good, shoot me and get me out of my misery'. He just couldn't stand those onions. You would have to go through living without a good warm meal for an extended period of time to appreciate this. He crawled back to his pup tent and got out a K ration.

He got a few pieces of a German mortar in his face and was awarded the Purple Heart. He was the Captains driver and he was to take the Captain to check a spot to cross the Roer River to take their equipment across. The Roer was a swift river where as the Rhine was a gentle flowing river. He stopped at the Army Headquarters and he went in to the Intelligence office to tell them where they were going. He was told that it was all clear. It was down in a valley and the Germans seen them go into the valley and they started lobbing mortars in. He was standing up in the seat of the jeep looking at a German reconnaissance plane circling around when a mortar round came in. He was in the middle of a road and next to a brick building where five G.I.'s were standing there and that mortar killed four of them. It blew him out of the Jeep behind the rear wheels so he figured that more would be coming in so he got up and ran across the road tripping over something and fell face first into a bomb crater. He tried to get up but his arms wouldn't hold him and he was bleeding profusely. A Captain hailed him and came down and turned him over and got out the sulpha powder and called for the Medics. He wound up in a big General Hospital in Waltenburg Holland. The Battle of the Bulge was in progress so it didn't matter if you were in the Airforce, Navy or whatever if you were considered able they took you out and you found yourself in the infantry. The day they were performing an operation on him he heard his Captain speak to the Colonel of the hospital that when this man is well enough to go back on duty he wanted them to be personally notified. He came back and got him or otherwise he would have ended up as one of those infantry replacements. Bodies for the Bulge.

Every year since the war he received a Christmas card from his Captain and after several years he knew he had moved to Kenesaw, Georgia so he got a hold of the Telephone operators and got his phone number. He called and a young man answered the phone and he asked 'is Marshall White there?' He asked who this is and Arnie said he served under his command during the war. He said he would rather not tell him his name at this time. The young man said to wait a minute and he heard him call out 'Grandpa it's for you'. A booming voice got on and Arnie said 'Captain White, do you know who this is?' He said 'say something else'. He mentioned several other words and the Captain said 'Arnold Bottger'. His Captain remembered him over all these years.

Viena Austria was divided into four sectors, French, Russian, British and American. Arnie and the Captain went into Viena and were properly arrested by the Russians. They claimed that they had strayed into their territory. They were held at the Russian headquarters for the best part of an hour. The Captain went up to the officer in charge and in no uncertain terms explained that he was an American officer and expected to be treated like one. They wanted his camera and he told them they could have his film but he sure wasn't going to give them his camera. Five minutes later they released them. They were just harassing them.

After the war was over they were in Austria and they went up one Sunday to Hitlers Eagles Nest. There was a foot path up to the nest and an elevator with a sign saying 'For the use of Field Officers of Major and above only'. They just got there when they heard a siren and here came a staff car with five stars, Eisenhower and Mark Clark. Eisenhower saw the sign and demanded to know who was responsible. Ike went over and yanked the sign out and threw it over the side of the mountain and said, 'everybody rides the elevator'. The nest wasn't too big and circular and a beautiful view of everything.

When coming home His unit boarded a Victory ship in Marseille on November 30, 1945. What a comparison to the Queen Elisabeth that they went over on. The main topic was 'do you get sea sick'. Arnie said 'no not me' and when in the Mediterranean it was OK but when they hit the Atlantic the ship broke down and they just bounced around like a cork in the water. Arnie got so sea sick that he was just laying in the bunk afraid that he was going to die, then he was afraid that he wouldn't. They landed in the United States December 13, 1945. He was discharged at Indiantown Gap, Pennsylvania December 18, 1945.

His decorations and citations consists of Good Conduct Medal, Purple Heart Medal, American Theatre Service Medal, European African Middle Eastern Campaign Medal with 3 bronze stars, Ruptured Duck Lapel Button.

Right after Arnie went into the service he had gotten married and about the third day after he arrived over seas he received a Dear John letter and ended up divorced.

His current wife's first husband was a school mate a year ahead of him. He was in the Air force and had one more mission to go when his plane was shot down from a direct hit. She had presented him with a son who he never got to see.

Arnie got out of the Army in 1945 and in November 27, 1946 he married Delilah Hatfield,(Wojnowski). He has one Stepson and they have a son and a daughter

Arnie retired in 1988 after 28 years as the Clerk of Newbury Township and four years as a Trustee.

MACK DENVER CANTERBURY

Mack D. Canterbury, 311 N. 3rd Street box 197, Rake, Iowa 50465

Born October 22, 1921 at Whites Creek, West Virginia

Mack left Buffalo W.Va. High School early to join the U.S. Army and received his diploma from Buffalo High School while in the service.

Mack enlisted in the U. S. Army at Fort Hayes, Ohio on January 6, 1940.

After boot camp he was assigned to the 18th Engineers at Fort Devins, Massachusetts.

In April of 1940 he said his unit was sent to Fort Benning, Georgia for maneuvers. He said they made the trip in the back of a dump truck with a canvas top and boards across the bed with no back rest. From Benning they went in the same type of transportation to Louisiana on maneuvers. They then left Louisiana and went to Fort Logan, Colorado.

In September his unit went to Camp McCoy, Wisconsin for maneuvers. After maneuvers they returned to Fort Logan in October.

In March of 1941 Mack's unit went to Vancouver Barracks, Washington traveling by way of New Mexico, Arizona, California and Oregon. In June of 1941 he went to Camp Hunter, Leggett, California for maneuvers. One month later In July Mack got orders to go to Hawaii and was assigned to the 804th Engineers. The Engineers job was to build runways. Mack said that there had to be a reason for that, which he soon found out.

Mack was at Pearl Harbor on that fateful day of December 7, 1941. He said that he was located in the Schofield Barracks next to Wheeler Field, both of which were close to where the attack occurred. He said that he heard an explosion that woke him up and he said that he got up and looked out the window and saw a plane coming toward them. It strafed them but they couldn't do anything because they didn't have any ammunition. They had used it all up on the rifle range the week before. After the Attack his 804th Engineers built over 20 airfields in the Hawaiian Islands. Then they were sent to build, repair and finish airfields at Baker Island, Maiken Island and Saipan Island.

He was returned to the states one month before V.J. day, September 2, 1945. He was assigned to Greensboro, North Carolina Recreation Center until it was time for him to go to Indian Town Gap, Pennsylvania for his discharge in October 1945.

After a short stint as a civilian Mack reenlisted in 1946 at Fort Meade, Maryland and was sent to the 313th Army Air Force BU in Greenville, South Carolina. From there Mack was transferred in January 1947 to the 463rd Army Air Force BU at Geiger Field, Washington.

His next assignment was the Military Police School at Carlisle Barracks, Pennsylvania. He then returned to the 463rd Army Air Force and his unit moved to Fort Francis E. Warren, Wyoming. While there he met and married Jean Ann Espeland 'a beautiful Norwegian girl' in Cheyenne, Wyoming. They were married November 15, 1947.

He was reassigned to the 3450th MP Squadron. In 1947 the Army Air Corp split and Mack joined the Air Force.

While in Wyoming Mack and his wife were blessed with two children, John Mack August 22, 1948 and Julia Lou November 16, 1949.

His military assignments with the 3450th MP Squadron were as follows.

21 January 1951   3650th AF Indoctrination Wing, Samson AFB, Geneva,
NY

9 February 1952 126th AP SQ, APO #16, Bordeaux, France where unit
moved to Laon, France, APO #17.

December 1952 The 126th AP Sq returned to the United States and
The 38th AP Sq was activated.

September 1953 768th AC&W Sq. Moriarty, New Mexico

September 1955 38th AP Sq, APO #17, Mack was to be sent back to Laon, France. The first time in France Mack didn't have his family along and this time he insisted his wife and kids be brought along. They arrived in December, 1955 traveling via USS General G.M. Randall from Fort Hamilton, New York. They lived on the French economy because housing was not available on base. While in Laon, France another son Eric D was born, March 28, 1956

June   1956 Mack attended the USAF Non Commissioned
Officers Academy at Friesing, Germany.

January   1957 Detachment #1, Headquarters 38th Bomb Group
TAC, APO #65, Landstuhl, Germany

April   1958   501st Tactical Control Wing, APO #65, Landstuhl,

Germany.

June   1958   616th AC&W Sqk, APO #35, Ulm, Germany

June   1959   3081st AP Sq, Rushmore AFS, Rapid City, South

Dakota. While in Rapid City another son was born,

David Alan February 23,1960.

Mack retired from the Air Force after 20 years, 6 months as a 1st, Sgt. E7 on September 30, 1961

Upon retirement the family settled down on their Century Home Farm in Rake, Iowa and it is still being managed and run by the youngest son David.

Evan though Mack retired from the service he still served his God and Country and was active in the American Legion, was a 40-year member of the Masonic Lodge and the Eastern Star, and was a proud member of the Pearl Harbor Survivors Association. Over the years he had been a Cub Scout Master, PTA President, and was involved in many other community services. He enjoys driving his military Jeep in parades, spending time at the farm and, most importantly, being with his family. He attended reunions when able keeping in contact with a number of his military friends.

His awards and medals consisted of – Army Commendation Medal, USAF Combat Readiness Medal, USAF Good Conduct Medal, American Defense Service Medal, WWII Occupation Medal, Asiatic Pacific Campaign Medal, American Campaign Medal, Victory Medal World War II, National Defense Service Medal, Ruptured Duck and several certificates of exemplary service.

His stint in the military took him to many locations in the Pacific, various posts around the states and a number of locations in Europe. He was a career Service Man and retired a Master Sergeant (E-7) enjoying his time in the service and proud of his accomplishments.

FRANK CRUTHERS, Jr

Frank Cruthers, Jr., 22435 W. Curtice Road, P.O. Box 146, Curtice, Ohio 43412-0146

Born July 30, 1926 in Cleveland, Ohio

Graduated from Tyrone High School, Tyrone, PA in 1945. Was drafted into the U.S. Army before graduation day and received his diploma while in the services.

He was drafted and taken by rail to Pittsburgh, PA for his induction. That's where he received his physical exam for entrance into the U.S. Army. He said that he had no one to see him off on the train like the others whose families were there wishing them well. He said that he remembered it being a very sorrowful time for him. From Pittsburgh they were taken to Indian Town Gap, PA where they were given their uniforms and other gear. He said that was where he got the best pair of shoes he had ever worn in his whole life.

Then on to Camp Wheeler, Georgia for boot training. One day his lieutenant called him to his side and asked him "What's the matter with those people in Pennsylvania? Do they think you're on a picnic? There's a war going on." Frank came to find out that his High School Principal had written to see if he might be allowed a leave of absence to go home to be with his graduating class for the Prom. Frank said he guessed the Principal wasn't thinking clearly.

After Basic training they were allowed 10 days leave so he went back to Bedford, PA to see his folks. When he got there the house was empty and he had to check with the neighbors to find out where they had gone. Low and behold his infant step-brother Robert had swallowed an open safety pin which had caught in his esophagus and they had taken him to the Mayo Clinic in Philadelphia to be operated on. He took a Greyhound Bus to Philadelphia and stayed with a relative while he checked with his family. He said that it was quite a sight to see this tiny baby connected to all sorts of tubes and wires to keep him alive. To small to remove the pin by going down his throat they had to open up his rib cage and take it out of there. The Doctors really performed a miracle that day since he is still alive today.

Upon leaving the hospital in uniform the last day of his leave to return to camp he was overrun by people running out into the streets. They were grabbing on to his uniform and clothing and the girls were all kissing him and cars were honking horns every where. Everyone was just going crazy! That's when he found out that it was VE Day and the Germans had surrendered.

He was to return to Fort Meade Maryland and when he got there his deployment was changed they were no longer going to be sent to Germany as planned but sent to Camp Rucker, Alabama for training in jungle warfare. He was trained in the use of a flame thrower and other jungle weaponry. After this training they were taken by troop train to Camp Roberts in the San Francisco Bay area for 8 days to learn how to swim. Then on the 24th of August 1945 they departed San Francisco on the U.S.S. GOSPER (A.P.A. 170) for the Philippines. The next day, August 25th, 1945, the Japanese surrendered while they were en route. They moved out under the Golden Gate Bridge into the Pacific and spent twenty two days zig-zagging across the Pacific to avoid any Japanese submarines that may be lurking about. A trip that would normally take only eight days to Luzon in the Philippines.

They arrived in the Philippines September 15 and found the entrance to Luzon blocked with sunken ships the

Lingayen Gulf so they had to ride in on LSD's to the beach. They spent about 1 ½ months in ideal conditions and quarters on the most beautiful sandy beaches and under huge towering palm trees that he had ever seen. Unfortunately there were also still Japanese soldiers high in the mountains above who had not received the news about the dropping of the Atomic Bombs and they were still shooting from their bunkers. The natives would bring fruits and vegetables or do menial chores for them, such as laundry or house cleaning in trade for the cigarettes and tropical chocolates we were issued. The things they coveted the most were the mattress covers we were issued which they in turn used as pullovers and clothing. The Philippine children would go crazy for the tropical chocolates which to him were the hardest on this earth.

Free beer was another issue they would receive and the fellows would bury it deep in the sands to keep it cold. One day while they were away from camp some of the Army soldiers who had been up in the hills were told the war was over and returned to base. Upon returning to the camp they discovered the beer, so they dug it up and put it in their tent. They found them setting on the beer saying it was theirs. It didn't look wise to challenge them. Two weeks later they were sent home.

Frank had never smoked in his 17 years on this earth. After getting their issue of free Lucky Strike cigarettes from the Sergeant one day the guys in his unit caught him and put him in the back of a 2 ½ ton truck and put the flaps down where they all began to light up. Then just to get his goat they all would blow the smoke at his face till he was gagging and turning green. What happened held the opposite effect of what they wanted. They wanted to get him started smoking. It actually turned him into an adamant non-smoker and to this day he can't stand being around cigarettes.

From the Philippines they were soon dispatched to Sasebo on the Honshu Island in Japan. Not knowing about a huge typhoon at sea they were caught up and about sunk. He remembers a big 1 ¾ ton truck onboard coming loose from it's moorings and sliding all over the deck which could have gone right through the hull of the ship. It took 15 guys to finally get it tied back down before it tore the ship apart. On Honshu Island they were to invade, but as luck would have it as they went ashore there stood the U.S. Marines who had already taken the place. They yelled and hooted and 'barked' at us as they landed making fun of the "dog faced" soldiers, a loving term they had for the U.S. Army.

Frank spent most of his time for over a year in Yamaguchi, Japan as a T5-Cpl Battalion Clerk. With the aid of a Japanese – American interpreter named Mary they were to procure any and all items they could lay their hands on from the Japanese to fix up and repair the old Japanese barracks and buildings used to house the American troops. They would bargain and trade for paint, wood, metal and other needed items. One day the Captain sent them to this warehouse on the outskirts of town to procure a new shipment of paint that had come in. The owner of the place became highly agitated that they were trying to confiscate his supply so the interpreter decided they should make a hasty departure from that endeavor.

Above Yamaguchi in the high mountains there were 360+ gun embankments with 22 inch thick concrete bunkers and underground tunnels built and dug by the Japanese some 20 years before in preparation for this war. Also ammunition storage units were built into the hills. To move this supply all work had to be done by human labor as no vehicles could maneuver around such steep cliffs. All the guns and other military gear was removed and taken by the US Army out to the middle of the Yellow Sea and dumped. One day his lieutenant let him do some scrounging around and he was able to send home several swords and a few other military souvenirs.

One weekend a buddy of Frank and he got a furlough to Tokyo where they decided they would go into one of the opium smoke dens to see what it was all about. After about 10 minutes of standing around and inhaling the smoke they felt like they had been smoking the stuff themselves. So they quickly got the hell out of there and never returned.

Finally towards the end of his hitch he was scheduled to return to the states. He left Yokahoma, Japan on September 19, 1946. He was loaded aboard one of the huge Victory Ships with a platoon of Negro troops and headed to Seattle, Washington arriving on September 29. On the way the seas were none too smooth and the fellows all bunked seven high below decks and became sick and were throwing up all over each other. Frank spent most of his journey above deck so he wouldn't get sick as well. For some reason they made them stand guard around the ship but he thought if someone wanted to leave the ship he sure as hell wasn't going to stop them. Where would they go but into the briny deep? By chance one day he ran into a guy named Stanley from Hickory Hill, PA who he had gone to school with back home in Defiance, PA. From then on until he was discharged from the Army they hung around together. But after that they never saw each other again. Strange how these things happen.

From Seattle they boarded a troop train back to Fort Meade, Maryland where he received his discharge on November 25, 1946.

He headed back home to Bedford, PA where his mother had opened a restaurant. She took all of his mustering out pay and bought him a suit and he started working with his brother at the Brady Barrel Stave factory.

He was not happy there so he soon headed to Cleveland, Ohio where he found his future wife Gloria Pinchot who was still going to high school. She was one of the few people including his father that wrote him on a regular basis while he was in the Army. Walking by her school one day she opened a second floor window and told him about the letter he sent her which had contained a large supply of stamps. She thought he really meant for her to make sure and write him but actually he had mistakenly put a letter in an envelope in which he kept his supply of stamps and unknowingly mailed it to her. Telling her was quite a let down but that must have had some unknown future meaning for them because they got married in September 1949.

They have four great children and many wonderful grandchildren and recently celebrated their 55th Wedding Anniversary.

His medals and citations consist of the EIB (expert infantry badge), Asiatic Pacific Medal, Japanese Occupation Medal, Good Conduct Medal, 32nd Infantry Presidential Citation, World War II Victory Medal, Ruptured Duck Lapel Pin and a certificate confirming crossing of the International Dateline.

After forty years and six months Frank retired from Sohio (now BP) in August 1989.

PAUL THOMAS DALE

Paul T. Dale, 6001 S. Comino De-Oeste, Tucson, Arizona 85746

Born December 24, 1928 in Belmont Co., Ohio

He attended school in East Cleveland, Ohio through the ninth grade.

Paul enlisted in the Army at the age of seventeen on January 6, 1946 by having a friend sign his mothers name on the permission papers. He went to Aberdeen Proving Grounds in Maryland where he went through boot camp. He fired marksman with the M1 rifle at the rifle range on the Chesapeake Bay.

Paul was sent to Camp Connaly Atlanta Depot, Georgia outside of Atlanta. There he was trained in medium automotive maintenance, trucks, jeeps and other automotive equipment. They would do something to the vehicles and then turn you loose to find out what was wrong and correct it. That was their means of training with correct supervision. He was in Company G, 2nd Regiment 9301 TSU Det 3 OTC Aberdeen Proving Grounds Maryland.

From there he was supposed to go to California and the South Pacific, which was where he wanted to go. He got to Camp Roberts, California where they ship troops out to the South Pacific and instead they put him on a train and sent him back to New York. They put him on a ship and sent him to Bremerhaven, Germany close to Bremen, Germany.

Once he arrived there they found that they had made a mistake and it was three months before he was sent back to the states. When he got back to the States they sent him to the Aberdeen Proving Grounds and had him training rookies. Then his mother contacted them informing them that she hadn't given her permission for his admittance in the military so they arranged his discharge.

He was discharge on December 7, 1946. His military career was a short one from January 4, 1946 to December 7, 1946 but during his time he earned the following medals – European, African, Middle Eastern Medal, World War 11 Victory Medal and Occupational Medal of Germany.

When Paul got back to the states He was given the job of training rookies at the Aberdeen Proving Ground boot camp. Paul was made duty NCO training new boots about the manual of arms and drill. He was still seventeen and younger than the ones he was training. He enjoyed his time in the service but when his mother arranged his discharge he decided not to fight it. One experience Paul had was with the Dentist. He told Paul that he had two teeth that needed to be pulled. Paul never had a tooth pulled so he asked the dentist if he could have just one of them pulled and if he took it alright he would come back for the other one. The Dentist agreed and he had the one tooth removed and came back later to have the second one removed.

His time and experiences in Germany were very interesting and he enjoyed all his time there and in the services. In going to Germany you travel the English Channel and pass the white cliffs of Dover and in the middle of the channel there were ships that were sunk and all you could see was their masts sticking out of the water. It was quite an experience for him.

Paul married Ann Dunning on October 24, 1969.

He retired from Kodecker Construction Company in 1986.

ANTHONY THOMAS DUDICH

Anthony Thomas Dudich, 14625 Zenith Drive, P.O. Box 156, Newbury, Ohio 44065.

Born in Cartaret, New Jersey, May 10, 1923
Family moved to Cleveland, Ohio when he was around three years old. Raised on 93rd and Union Avenue. Tony went to Parochial Nativity through the 8th grade, Nathan Hale in the 9th grade then to John Adams High school in Cleveland quitting in the eleventh grade to get a job.

Enlisted in the Marine Corp in March 1943 and went straight to San Diego Marine Recruiting Depot. At that time the East Coast Base was quarantined with a spinal meningitis epidemic. He took his rifle range practice at both Camp Mathews and Camp Elliot. He made Expert Marksmanship but usually displayed the sharpshooter pin because it's a better looking one. He's handled the 30 caliber garand M1, the M1 Carbine, B.A.R., the Colt 45,

Tommy Gun and 30 Caliber light & heavy Machine guns. As expert he received five dollars a month extra. Then he went on to advanced training in a tent area at Camp Pendleton, Salito canyon and every time it rained they were in deep mud.

They shipped out from San Diego straight to the Marshall Islands. They went straight into combat at the island of Kwajalein, It was the first time that a division went straight from the states into battle and it was the first Japanese territory captured in world war two. He was a part of the Fourth Marine Division, 25th Regiment. He landed there on January 30,1944 and the island was secure by February 5th,1944. They landed on Roi Island by the airport. Roi had the airport and Namur had the hospital and other buildings and the ammunition dump. A blockhouse was mistakenly identified and it was filled with torpedo warheads and aerial bombs and when his outfit destroyed it, it caused an explosion that killed both Japanese and American troops. The first or second day the Japanese planes came over the island and dropped tinsel which was used to mess up radar tracking. The second run they came over and laid their eggs   Tony and his friend discussed the necessity of digging a foxhole thinking they could hide behind some rocks but after the bombing run they decided they had better dig a foxhole immediately.   Over on one section of the island the Japanese had a couple of 5 in. guns and across the island in the ocean was a cruiser and they were shooting back and forth right over their positions at each other. One of his buddies, Buddy (Robert) Coons was digging a foxhole and he went to pick up his shovel raising it up above his hole and one of the Japanese shells ricocheted off his shovel and went tumbling about five hundred yards into the lagoon and exploded. Buddy was killed later on Saipan. They stayed on the island for about a month until the Army came and relieved them. During the month from dead bodies, etc. hordes of flies came and we came down with dysentery. The flies were very daring, they would land on your dish when eating and you couldn't shoo them off. You had to take your finger and flip each one off individually. The Army had quite a task with all their heavy machinery burying bodies and cleaning up the island.

From there they went to Maui for more training. They practiced different exercises all over the island. Then they were boarded aboard ships without being told where they were going until they were well on their way. They were shown maps and briefed about the island of Saipan that they were going to hit next.

On June 15th they boarded landing craft and hit the beaches of Saipan. His unit hit the area adjacent to Aslito Airfield. Saipan took 30 days to secure. Then they went back aboard ship managed to clean up and get some good food. On July 24th they hit Tinian. There was only one area that they could land on Tinian and it was so heavily mined and covered with coral reefs that the landing crafts, Alligators, couldn't get through. He jumped out to get to shore and sunk well over his head losing his M1. He had to dive down to recover his weapon then continue on to the beach. They were under heavy fire with machine gun bullets hitting all around him. He managed to hide between the coral reefs that were sticking up like tree trunks. He managed to get to the beach where 'all hell broke lose.' Sgt. Goldstein & Joe Silverman were a couple of Jewish members of his outfit. There weren't many Jews around but these two were good Marines. Joe Silverman got hit by friendly fire and a piece of shrapnel went through his back and came out of his stomach. He later died. He use to attend the Chaplain's Catholic service with him and he'd say it's one God. Joe always complained that he was too old and shouldn't be there, he was thirty years old. Sgt. Goldstein was with him on Tinian behind a man made hill that ran the length of the beach. They were on one side of the hill and the Japanese was on the other side. The Japanese were throwing hand grenades over the hill to their side and they were throwing them back. One of the grenades finally hit Tony on the neck and the cheek of his ass. A minor hit but he couldn't walk because it stuck to his cheek. They were traveling along the hill and came to an opening between two sections of the hill. Sgt Goldstein ran into the opening Tony seen a muzzle flash and the Sgt. Got shot right in the stomach. He was right in front of him and when he got shot he flew backwards about ten feet. He and the Sgt. both fired and got the one who shot him. They went ahead and went up to the airfield #1 (where the Enola Gay took off) and they got into about the center of the airfield when the Japanese machine guns opened up and started cutting them all down. When O'Malley got hit in the biceps Tony was next to him and he started to screaming and Tony drug him out with bullets shooting all around him. They finally got Tony through the leg. He dragged O'Malley behind a big boulder and another guy came up and said that a fellow Marine was lying out there all shot up in the belly. He ran down and grabbed him and the Marine was a monster big and tall with him only about 150# trying to drag him out. O'Malley was bitching about the pain so he gave him morphine that he had. Getting back to the beach we were like two drunks staggering with their wounds trying to make the beach. He saw Sgt. Goldstein lying there on a stretcher all yellow, looking like he was dead. They got aboard ship and had their wounds bandaged up. They put this Goldstein in a refrigerated compartment because he was dead, about three days later the corpsman went to place some one else in the refrigerator when Goldsteins hand fell out. They took him out and he was alive! He went down to Espirito Santas, New Hebrides island hospital and then hop scotching back to Maui went on different ships that took them to a Guadalcanal Hospital and then to another little hospital in the Solomon Islands. Then they went back to Honolulu to a Navy Hospital and there was Sgt Goldstein still alive. Tony was sent back to his outfit and went through the same old training that they laughingly liked to call R and R, more training and then went to Iwo Jima.

On February 19,1945 they hit the beaches of Iwo Jima. Tony said that in 13 months they had four major operations. February of '44 to January of '45. Tony hit the beach on the first wave, in fact he was in the first wave of every operation. He said our Colonel was gung ho and volunteered them for every thing. They hit the beach, sinking up to their shins in the black volcanic ash. Tanks would belly out in the black ash within 20 or 30 feet. One tank near him was stuck and the turret opened up and a guy arose out with a tommy gun and it must have been a direct shell hit the tank turret for in one second nothing but a puff of smoke. Tony said the Japanese had the best artillery men on Iwo Jima in the whole Japanese Army. An LCI (landing craft infantry) was coming in and Japanese artillery made a direct hit on the pilot house, troops were jumping overboard all over. Tony was only on Iwo Jima one day. There was a sunken ship and Japanese snipers were on it and his friend Sonny Hudson went to say something to him when a bullet hit him right between the eyes – he was dead before he hit the ground. He said that he got about a mile inland when they cut loose with their daisy cutters, machine guns and every thing they had taking every one down. They went to a place they called the meat grinder where he got hit twice. Big trench dug out, tank trench, ten foot wide, on the left side was a wall it was like a cliff but it had little holes in it and snipers were shooting through these holes. They were picking us all off because they were up on top and shooting down on us. They lost more than half the platoon right there. A Jap on the other side of the trench threw a grenade at him and he laid down. The grenade went off and he prepared to fire at the Jap when he raised up to throw another grenade but eight times the rifle failed to go off. He figured it was a broken firing pin. Right now that rifle is sitting about a mile out from Iwo Jima, he deep sixed it. The Jap finally got him; in fact some of the shrapnel is still in him. At the same time a sniper got him, the bullet went through the stock of his rifle, through his arm, through his cartridge belt and cut four bullets in half and kept on going. Tony said that both his arms became numb. He went aboard ship where they just laid him on a table and took a knife and cut all his clothing off, even his shoe strings, then they peeled him off just like a cabbage. Then they checked you all over and dressed you up. It was just a troop transport ship that they used as an emergency hospital ship. They had a refrigerator where they kept a lot of the bodies until they could bury them at sea. That was his ticket home. He said "you know I didn't even think about it, I don't know if we were stupid, naïve or what but I didn't even think about getting killed, wounded or anything, nothing ever bothered us". He had both arms in slings across his chest and he was out on the deck when it was just starting to get dark when the air raid sirens went off. Bombers were coming about the second or third day on Iwo and he was stuck on deck. The sailors ran inside and locked the hatches and he was unable to open the hatch to get inside with both his arms all bound. So he was watching all the little Higgins boats running around laying smoke screens between all these ships and all around, pretty soon he heard the bombers coming and laying there bombs right next to the ship with water flying over board and getting him all wet. He had to duck behind a gunnel, he couldn't get back in. The following day he saw the flag go up on Mt. Suribachi. From there he went back to a hospital on Tinian. Almost back to the same place he had been hit twice before. He was there for a couple of days when he got his first airplane ride in a C-47 that took him from Tinian to a hospital in Guam. There you slept all day and was up all night with a 45 under your pillow. The Japs would come in from the hills at night and slice all the patients throats. He was glad to get off that island, too. He went from there to Honolulu then back to San Francisco. Tony said it was June by then and he was pretty well healed. They gave him a months furlough then they sent him up to the Boston Navy Yard. He said that is where he lost his stripes. He was up for Sgt., when, as he put it, he was talking to one of his girl friends in the guard house when Admiral Felix Gygax drove thru his gate and he wasn't there to properly enter him. So he lost his bid for Sgt.

On February 28th, 1946 he received his discharge at the Boston Navy Yard. His parents were back in New Jersey so he joined them there.

Some of his closest buddies were –
Tom O'Malley, Iron Mike

"Doc" Masotta
Roy Dewey
Sonny Hudson, sniper killed him on Iwo.
Corporal Gervalis
Biagio (Gene) Maddelena
Ted Kelce

His medals consist of the Bronze Star, two Purple Hearts, Asiatic Pacific Medal with four stars, American Theatre, Victory Medal and copies of two Presidential Unit Citations.

In 1948 he married Sylvia Caffery and they had three daughters and a son, Shelley the baby, Jackie and Patty the oldest girl, Thomas the son. He has ten grandchildren and three great grandchildren.

Tony worked for Clark Controller and National Barrel and Steel. He retired from Clark Controller.

After retiring from Clark Controller he worked driving school busses for Newbury Schools for two years and then one year with Headstart School.

He belongs to the Veterans of Foreign Wars, Disabled American Veterans, Marine Corp League, Fourth Marine Division Association and Geauga Memorial Foundation.

He is presently the Commander of the Newbury VFW Post 1068 and Geauga County Veterans Affairs

Commissioner. It's a part of GOVA, Governors Office Veterans Affairs, composed of eighty eight counties and eighty eight Veterans Affairs. GOVA started back during the Civil War.

RICHARD FRANKLIN FOGEL

Richard F. Fogel, 27 Sycamore Drive, Olmsted Township, Ohio 44138

Born in Cleveland, Ohio February 17, 1923.

Graduated from West Technical High School in 1941

Enlisted in the Marine Corp Air Force January 4, 1942 at Dallas, Texas.

He went to boot camp at San Diego and the rifle range at Camp Mathews.

He attended service school at El Toro, California, and took a course in Rockets and Fuses. His principal military duty became Armorer of Aircraft, SSN 911.

His service consisted of arming various aircraft in parts of various Marine Air Wings. He wouldn't be involved in ground contact with the enemy but some of his locations would still be in vulnerable strafing, bombing areas. Some of his duties would be aboard aircraft carriers and ground locations where airfields would be secured. As the war advanced across the Pacific Islands and airfields were secured his units would operate from them. He may not have been in physical combat but in arming planes in the units he was stationed with and becoming familiar with the young pilots it could become just as traumatic. As the planes would leave on missions and a count would be made as they leave they would nervously await the count on their return. Any pilots not returning from a mission would be very traumatic to the ground crew.

Richards records showed his unit served the following operations –

> 1st. Marine Div. – Guadalcanal/Tulagi from August thru December 1942
> 2nd Marine Div. – Tarawa in November 1943
> 3rd Marine Div. - Empress Augusta Bay Beachhead, Bougainville from November 1st to December 22, 1943.
> 1st Marine Div. - Supporting 11th Marines – Cape Gloucester from December 26, 1943 to April 30, 1944

4th Marine Div. - Saipan & Tinian from June 15 to
   August 1, 1944
3rd Marine Regiment – Guam July 21 to August 10,
   1944
1st Marine Div - Peleliu and Ngesebus, Palau
   Islands from September 15 to 29, 1944.
1st and 6th Marine Div. – Okinawa, Shima &
   Ryukus from April 1 to June 21, 1945
2nd, 4th and 5th Marine Div. – Iwo Jima from
   February 19 to 28, 1945.

This would represent the basic major operations that he had a hand in participating in. His various air units served also at, Munda, Northern Solomons, Vella Lavella, Torokina, Gilbert Islands, Marshall Islands, Marianas Islands, Linguyan Gulf and Manila Area.

He returned to the States to Marine Corp Air Station at Miramar, San Diego, California where he received his discharge June 7th, 1946.

He retired with the Rank of Sergeant.

His medals consisted of American Campaign Medal and Asiatic-Pacific Campaign Medal. Ruptured Duck lapel pin.

He married Miss Arlene Gutzman on October 26, 1956
They had two children, two girls.
He retired from his business, R. F. Printing Service.

RONALD WAYNE GRASSETTE

RONALD WAYNE GRASSETTE,417 Balsam
Street,Elmira, New York 14904

He was born in Cambridge, Mass. December 25, 1945

He graduated high school at Ridge-Latin High School

His father was a disabled veteran of WWII in Europe

He was drafted into the Army on June 10th, 1968
and went to Fort Dix, N.J. for his basic training. He spent
eight weeks in boot camp and three weeks of leadership
training in radio. They thought maybe he could be a
leader. From there he went to Fort Gordon, Georgia. He
spent ten weeks in radio/teletype training. A crash

course. He went straight from Fort Gordon via United Airlines to Fort Lewis in Washington. He embarked from Fort Lewis, via United Airlines with a few stop overs, to Ben Hoa Vietnam arriving January 1969. At Ben Hoa he became attached to the 101st Airborne Division, 1st Bn. 501st Infantry. They gave us some orientation and then shipped us to Hue, LZ Sally base camp. Vietnam was broken up into three sections, Ist Corp, 2nd Corp and 3rd Corp. Ist Corp was in northern part of Vietnam, 2nd Corp was in middle half and 3rd Corp was in southern tip of Vietnam. He was in Ist Corp near the DMZ.

The first action he seen was in Chu Lai. The base camp was overrun with 80% casualties. He saw his first enemy and American casualties there. One of his friends in the outfit, Bob Johnson, they use to call him stretch, they were on a recon patrol. They were following a trail when they ran into a series of booby traps so Sgt Anderson said they had better leave the trail. They started crossing a rice patty and as soon as they got half way across the rice patty all hell broke loose. We started to get mortar rounds and machine gun fire. The firing lasted about five minutes and he called in the medevac and gunships and as soon as they came in the VC took off. As he turned around Stretch received a direct hit with a mortar round. One second he was there and the next second, nothing. The VC knew that when the booby traps were spotted that it would divert us toward the rice patty so they were all zeroed in awaiting us. There were ten in the patrol and they ended up with two killed and two wounded. The first enemy casualties he seen was by a sapper attack, about eight VC that came into their perimeter and they tripped up a flare and they just opened up on them and that is where he saw his first enemy casualties. There were two in each bunker, one had a machine gun and the other had a grenade launcher. Ron had a grenade launcher and he got two with one shot. They were wiped out before they got into the perimeter where they liked to get inside and get to the communication area, mess hall and wherever they good cause the most casualties. Chu Lai was a fire base that they were just rebuilding. Opening up the area from trees, etc. so they could have a good fire zone. One night they hit us with every thing they had, first round was mortars, rockets and moved in their troops. Sappers they called them carrying in explosives. They had to retreat but they had a prepared area that was mined, but they knew exactly where to go to an area where choppers came in and picked them up. An escape route. He was a radio operator that called in the evacuation helicopters and directed artillery fire.

At Hue and fire base at Phu Vang he was the radio operator the troops would call and he would call in the Medevac and Gunships to go where needed. He worked as liaison with the South Vietnamese Army. He traveled with them and they would give him their positions that he would chart on the maps. Any time they got into a firefight and they needed Medevac, Gunships or artillery support he would call in for them. He had an interpreter next to him that would tell him what they would need. He would contact LZ Sally and they would send in Medevac's, gunships or whatever they would need. That's where he spent most of his time. He said that the Vietnamese Army were not very good, they would often in the middle of a firefight throw down their weapons and run. While there they had a Vietnamese family that did everything for them. They cleaned their huts, washed their clothes and prepared their food. He became very attached to a young Vietnamese girl and toyed with the thought of taking her back to the states. One night the North Vietnamese infiltrated their positions and the next day the family was gone and never found again.

Later he was returned to Hue as a radio operator. When he had about three months left they were going to send him to the rear, to Ben Hue. He was being transported by helicopter when the helicopter was shot down by a hand held rocket. They were shot down and landed right in a rice patty. They all survived the crash thanks to the pilots expertise. At about a hundred yards to their left there was a lot of vegetation area. They all took off to hide and the thing was that in their hurry they neglected to take along the radio. They all panicked and ran and had no way of calling in for support. He took it upon himself to run back to the helicopter under fire, grabbed the radio and ran back to cover. He called in and they got fire support and wiped out the VC and then sent in the choppers and removed them to safety. That is where he got the Bronze Star.

In Vietnam there wasn't any front line, when we took ground we never kept it. It was always a group of thirty or forty having a fire fight, always trying to find them. They were constantly moving all over Vietnam chasing them and very seldom getting them in the open. It was just guerrilla warfare. Occasionally they would make mistakes and you would get them in the open but normally they were very hard to find. Most damage was caused by artillery, air strikes, napalm and rockets. He said that all the time he was over there he had only seen action twice. That meant being shot at. He said that you could go weeks or months without being shot at and that the biggest offensive was the Tet Offensive of '68.

He was in a fire base, building a base about ten clicks from the DMZ, the most northernmost fire base in Vietnam. As they were doing this they could see the planes out in the perimeter spraying the agent orange on the vegetation. One day they were filling sand bags when they felt this slime all over their bodies. He guessed the wind blew the agent orange all over them. Back then he didn't think any thing of it, they just took a shower and that was it. That was how he got in contact with agent orange.

On January 17, 1970 he was discharged from Fort Dix, New Jersey. He continued in the Army reserves until June 9th, 1974. His rank at time of discharge was E-4 (Corporal).

The medals he earned were, **Bronze Star**, National Defense Service Medal, Army Commendation Medal, Vietnam Service Medal and Republic of Vietnam Campaign Medal with two o/s bars.

He married Carolyn Anita Cruthers in 1972 at Winchester, Mass. He is now the proud father of two daughters and one granddaughter.

Moved to Elmira, N.Y. in 1986 and ended up in the Buffalo, N.Y. V.A. Hospital in 1994 where he was diagnosed with Agent Orange which leaves him 100% disabled. He came down with it in August, 1994. He ended up in the Veterans Administration Hospital in Buffalo, N.Y. At that time his whole body practically shut down. His wife was warned that he might not survive. He managed to come out of it but physically impaired.   They told him they wanted to try an experiment with him - he had nothing to loose at this point. He don't know exactly what they did because he was drowning in his own fluids and after they were done he was able to relieve himself of all this fluid and recovered. His kidney's had shriveled up to nothing and after he had lost all that weight his kidneys came back 100%. Within a week he was feeling great, that was one experiment that really worked.

His closest friend was a George Pappas that went through high school with him, was drafted with him and was with him all the time he was in the service, came back to the states with him and discharged along with him. Very unusual to have any one you are very close to being with you every step of the way. He was in infantry.

Sometimes when transporting troops back and forth he would serve as a gunner on the Helicopters. They would transfer troops from LZ Sally to ambush positions and return. They would be supported by gunships that would circle the perimeter to protect them. He fired a few times but never at any particular target, just at covering locations. Later a body count would be made of the location but he had no knowledge of him ever hitting anyone. He personally never experienced hand to hand combat.

J. MICHAEL GROSS

J. Mike Gross, 5754 Township Road 351, Millersburg, Ohio 44654

He was born July 29, 1950 in Equality, Illinois.

They moved to St Petersburgh, Florida where he graduated from Northeast High School in 1968.

He joined the Marine Corp in August 1969 on a delayed entry and reported for active service on November 25th, 1969.

Before Mike entered active service he married his High School Sweetheart, Miss Lynn V. Fruehwirth on September 5th, 1969.

He received his Boot training at Paris Island, North Carolina and his infantry training at Camp Geiger, South Carolina.

Mike was then sent to the Marine Corp Recruit Training Depot in San Diego, California where he received Technical School Training in Communications.

His first post was May 24 1970 in Hawaii where he worked in communication service. With Marine Air Group 24 in Kaneohe Bay, Hawaii where he received his promotion to Sergeant.

After three successful years the Marine Corp moved him all the way back to Cherry Point, North Carolina where he served in the message center with Marine wing communication Squadron 28. While at Cherry Point he was deployed to sea for six months aboard USS Manitowac County. LST-28 While at North Carolina he received his appointment as Staff Sergeant.

After that tour he got to do something a little different, he was a special weapons technician for ground war nuclear weapons Two years at Twenty Nine Palms and One year at Okinawa.

After that tour he went to Camp Pendleton where he served with the Ninth Communication Battalion as skilled message center chief. He served in

Communications for major commands for the Fleet Marine Force Pacific. Mike was promoted as Gunnery Sergeant with this command.

The next assignment was 1st Battalion 11th Marines, at Camp Pendleton. He was the Communication Chief for an artillery battalion. An artillery battalion has twice as many people and twice the amount of equipment as an infantry battalion.

Mike said that ever since he had entered the Marine Corp he always wanted to be an Embassy Marine, a Marine assigned to the Marine detachment to guard one of the Embassies around the world. Except for the senior position of Staff NCO in charge of the detachment, every Marine had to be single. He was married when he came into the Marine Corp so he wasn't qualified until the time he made Staff Sergeant. Then he was qualified to become the Senior Staff NCO. When he was assigned to the 1st. Battalion 11th Marines he had the opportunity to work under his Commanding Officer, Colonel Blaise and as it happens he had been a former officer in charge of Marine Detachments in a prior tour of his. Because of Mike's exceptional job under his command he was in position to ask him for a recommendation to be assigned to a Marine Embassy Detachment. He didn't yet have orders applying to that but he was going to recommend him and he was looking forward to his next career of duty being to an Embassy duty. At the same time the Marine Corp recognized they had a need for recruiters in the recruiting field. The Commandant of the Marine Corp created a special board of Marines to travel from base to base to look for possible candidates to be recruiters. As they interviewed they weren't looking for volunteers because they were basically looking for who would qualify. They were issuing orders based on that. When they came to Camp Pendleton California they reviewed everybody's military records to determine who they wanted to talk to. Naturally he was selected to be interviewed. They couldn't find any reason in his records that would disqualify him so they told him that he could expect orders for recruiting duty. That effectively killed any chance of getting orders for Embassy duty at that time. Even though Mike told them that he had planned for Embassy Duty they had advised him that the Commandant had given them priority over any one they chose and there was no way to get out of those orders. The only way he could have gotten out would have been to disqualify himself and when orders came down to his Commanding Officer he had to approve them, this was the same Commanding Officer that was going to send him to Embassy Duty, and he asked him whether he should approve them or not. He effectively could have disapproved them based on some disqualification of his. He asked him what he should do and Mike said that he really didn't want to go on recruiting duty, his heart was set on Embassy Duty, but he didn't want it to go on his official military records that he wasn't qualified to do anything. Mike was young and cocky and felt that he could do anything the Marine Corp wanted so he put down that he was qualified. So Mike was sent out on recruiting duty for three years in Pittsburgh, Pennsylvania. Mike claimed that it was the hardest three years that he had in his entire Marine Corp service. He was successful at it and he completed his tour but it was difficult for many other reasons. Primarily because you were no longer in the military environment, you were now working in the civilian community and it was a whole different set of rules. Your success was no longer based on how good a job you do but on the base of the young man you are talking to, whether he will join the service or not.

If you were considered successful in your recruiting duty and served your whole three years as an award you were given the opportunity to select your next assignment. That's how he got his next assignment in Norfolk, Va. To the Admirals staff for the Commander in chief U. S. Forces Atlantic where he served as Communications Supervisor in the command center and war room. He was stationed there for three years.

Next he went over to become Communications Operations Chief for the G6 Division for the Commanding General fleet Marine Force, Atlantic. There he served the balance of his time of about a year and a half until he retired.

He retired and was provided with a full retirement ceremony at Norfolk, Virginia with full military honors. The ceremony was performed by his Commanding Officer Colonel Palmquist.

Medals, citations and accolades received were-

Nations Commendation Medal to Master Sergeant J. M. Gross, United States Marine Corp. for service as set forth in the following citation. For meritorious service while servicing as G6 operation chief, Headquarters, Fleet Marine Corp Atlantic from 31 December 1988 to 30 May 1990. During this period Master Sergeant Gross performed his duties in an outstanding manner. Due to his superb management and technical skills he managed to contribute significantly to the accomplishment of the G6 mission in many areas. He aggressively implemented new soft ware applications with streamlined section procedures that saved valuable resources. He developed and improved administrative and accountability procedures for the classified document Secretary control point that set the standard for the force headquarters. As the project officer involved in operational testing of the circuit satellite testing and single channel gravity air radio systems he provided sound recommendations and intelligence elevating courses of action. The outstanding leadership displayed by Master Sergeant Gross contributed directly to the forces present and future ability to communicate successfully. This superlative achievements concluded a distinguished career over twenty years of loyal and thankful service to his country. By his initiative and selfless devotion to duty, Master

Sergeant Gross upheld the highest traditions of the Marine Corp and the United States Naval Service.
For the Secretary of the Navy, F. A. Hughey, Brigadier General, U. S Marine Corp, Deputy Commander Fleet Marine Force Atlantic.

From Commanding General Fleet Marine Force to Master Sergeant Gross, USMC. Subject Transfer to the Fleet Marine Corp Reserve You are transferred to the Fleet Marine Corp Reserve effective 31 May 1990. You are released from active duty at twenty four hundred on the effective date of your transfer and will resume your status on the Fleet Marine Corp Reserve on the following day. As of 31 May 1990 you have completed twenty years ten months and twelve day of cumulative service of which twenty years six months and twenty day as active service. Your presence will be missed by your fellow Marines. On the behalf of the Commandant of the Marine Corp and those of whom you served I express sincere appreciation for your service and wish you health and happiness in every success in the future. E. T. Cook, Jr., lieutenant General U. S. Marine Corp, Commanding.

Dear Master Sergeant Gross the Marine Corp has been your occupation and family for many years past. Now I am certain memories, interest and the future of the Corp will remain with you forever. In your desire to obtain your accomplished goals you have fully demonstrated the exceptional leadership qualities and professional contributions we seek of our senior Marines. We are

proud as you must be of your most successful career. As a teacher of young Marines, a source of wise council and as an example of those virtues we so admire you have made a mark on the Corp that will remain long after you have left our active ranks. There are many young Marines you have influenced who will carry on in the same fine tradition always characterized by the United States Marine Corp. You have my best wishes for good health and success in the years ahead.
Sincerely, A. M. Gray, General U. S. Marine Corp., Commandant of the U. S. Marine Corp.

Dear Master Sergeant Gross, on the occasion of your retirement from active service I would like to extend my appreciation for your more than twenty years of loyal and dedicated service. Your leadership, professional ability and unwavering devotion to duty have upheld the finest tradition of our Corp. On behalf of the personnel of the Fleet Marine Force Atlantic I wish you many years of success and happiness. Sincerely, E. T. Cook Jr., Lieutenant General U. S. Marine Corp., Commanding General Fleet Marine Force Atlantic.

Mikes wife Lynn was then ushered to the front beside him and honored thusly.
The United State Marine Force certificate of appreciation is presented to Lynn V. Gross on the occasion of the retirement of your spouse from active duty. You have earned the Marine Corps appreciation for your unselfish, faithful and devoted service. Your unfailing support and

understanding has made possible for your spouses lasting contribution to a grateful nation. Given by my hand this 31st day of May, 1990 E. T. Cook, Jr. Lieutenant General U. S. Marine Corp., Commanding General Fleet Marine Force Atlantic.

Mike and his wife Lynn were blessed with two children, John Michael born during his tour in Hawaii and Judy Lynn born during his tour in Okinawa.

His decorations, medals, badges, citations and campaign ribbons awarded or authorized were - Rifle badge sharpshooter, Pistol badge expert, Good conduct medal with six stars, Joint service commendation medal, Sea service deployment ribbon, Navy unit commendation, Meritorious unit commendation, National defense service medal, Meritorious Mast and Two letters of appreciation.

His rank at time of discharge on May 31, 1990 was Master Sergeant Technical, Pay grade E-8.

Many enduring associations were formed along the way and shared with his wife and family.

His training and experience is carried over in his civilian life as a Computer Technologist with his sons company J. M. Gross Consulting.

ALBERT J. HUMPHREY

Albert J. Humphrey, 2890 Cedar Hill Road, Cuyahoga Falls, Ohio 44223

Born September 27,1922 at Akron, Ohio

Graduated from North High School, Akron, Ohio
He attended Akron University prior to being drafted.

After Pearl Harbor he went up to Cleveland and attempted to enlist in the Navy and they rejected him because of a bridge he had in the front of his mouth. They said, "no it won't do". When he got home his mother was upset that he had tried to join, and his father was upset because he had attempted to join the Navy because his father was in the Army in France. He waited until he was drafted into the Army on December 10, 1942.

A contingent went by train to Fort Hayes in Columbus, Ohio. All draftees from Ohio, Pennsylvania and West Virginia. They were in Fort Hayes a few days.

He has written about his experience there and the fact that they hadn't slept for 36 hours before they were required to take an I.Q. test. He was lucky to get 110. 110 or above you could apply for OCS, but they were put in with a bunch of fellows from the South with an I.Q. of 47. They got rid of some of those later on. He tried to get into the Air Corps but nobody would listen to him. A fellow he graduated with from North High School was there and he had gone to the orderly room to telephone when he overheard an officer and a first sergeant talking about a message they had just received saying that everybody was going down to Camp Van Dorn, Miss. to a new activation of the 99th Div. They ended up down there in tar paper shacks. He did his boot training at Camp Van Dorn, Mississippi. His training was with the Infantry and he handled the M1 and carbine. His expertise was with the M1. After 13 weeks of basic training he was fortunate to get a job in the supply room with a Corporal rating. This was G Company 394th Infantry, 99th Division (Checkerboard)

They had their boot training at Camp Van Dorn and performed some maneuvers in Louisiana.

On November 19,1943 they were transferred to Camp Maxey, Texas where he took his advanced training. It was a beautiful set up with a two story barracks and indoor plumbing.

German POW's from the desert area were brought into Texas and Louisiana. We saw them not close enough to talk to, but some of them were living on our base. But we were kept apart from them. They were so suntanned, they all wore shorts, and they all looked so husky. They were eating better than we were. We did not get milk, or ice cream and they were paid if they worked. They got ten cents an hour and they could get cigarettes and some of them could even get into town. They never had it so good. That's the reason so many of them came back to this country after the war.

He tried to get into the Air Corps and went over to Sherman, Texas to take a test. 450 people were there. He was the last one to turn his paper in and they said you failed – they said you failed yourself because you tried too hard. From then on he made up his mind that he was going to be in the infantry. He said that he became a better soldier – perhaps.

They trained at Camp Maxey, Texas. Lt. General Lesley J. McNair of the Army in Washington, D.C. viewed us after maneuvers. General Eisenhower wanted us, but General McNair kept us for more training. General Eisenhower had bad feelings about this and later on when he wrote a book he didn't want to recognize the 99th Division. Supply Sgt. Waters was transferred to Battalion. Albert got his job as Supply Sgt. Forms WD32 were for clothing and WD33 for equipment issued each man, including Rifle, BAR or Carbine and serial numbers. Statement of Charges came into use rather quickly, with the breakage of Post Camp & Station crockery in the Mess Hall. It wasn't the cost as much as the blemish on a GI's record to be charged so those in HQ Platoon were convinced to take turns and accept the Statement of Charges. He established friends at Regimental Supply and had many unaccounted for pieces of clothing and equipment to give a GI in need.

After his advanced training he was sent to his port of embarkation at Camp Miles Standish, Boston on September 13, 1944. On October 10, 1944 he landed in Gourock, Scotland and sent by train to Southern England. Arriving at Aubel, Belgium November 14th we removed our shoulder patches as ordered since we were a "Secret Div.". We then moved on line, relieving the 9th Division and covering a thinly held front of 22 miles. The German loud speakers welcomed the 99th Division, therefore spoiling the "secret" arrival. It was a quiet front for a month with daily patrols going out, receiving occasional shelling and "Buzz Bombs". Our Mail clerk, Victor Tiziani, was our first KIA.

The men of the 99th. Division were on the line from November 11 and the Battle of the Bulge started

December 16th. The men wore out a lot of gloves cutting trees and logging over their holes building shelters. C.O. John Haymaker, told him to requisition 137 pairs of gloves. He jeeped over to regimental supply, finding it in a brick school building. He entered a large, heated room. Everyone was quietly, with heads bent, doing paperwork. As he approached each man he'd known for two years, with requisition in hand, they nodded their head to the next rank and file, ignoring his greeting. Warrant Officer Botts was the only absentee. Sitting at a desk, on a raised platform, was the S-4 Major. Albert approached him with the requisition. The Sgt. Major ignored it and demanded a "statement of charges against every man," to account for the necessity of replacing the requisitioned items. Albert replied, "These items were expendable in a combat area." The Sgt. Major again demanded a statement of charge. Albert then asked if the Sgt. Major would accept a "Report of survey" for lost or destroyed articles. The Sgt. Major ordered him to leave, threatening to call the MPs.

Arriving back at the kitchen area in Murringen, He found Sgt. Jerry Holloway waiting. Sgt. Holloway wanted Albert to see his F Company supply down the road. Walking down, they were surprised by a couple of old civilian men jumping out from behind a house shaking their fists at us. Jerry told him to ignore them.

That day he went to the front lines with the hot chow jeep and trailer. Albert was talking with the first sergeant when a shell came in, wounding him in the leg, and driver Guthrie Harlow in the shoulder. Shrapnel went through his overcoat between his legs, missing him, and taking a chunk out of his carbine stock. He dropped to the ground. Huley Wooten, sitting on a GI water can that was spewing water from shrapnel holes, grabbed his mess kit and shoveled food in his mouth. Nerves and shock do strange things. At a reunion, Elvin Beckerman also remembered this occurrence.

The next morning Sgt. Waters picked him up by jeep, telling him they would look for 1st. Sgt. Buzinski, who was hospitalized with a shrapnel wound received on December 4th. They drove all day –Malmedy, Eupen, etc. Albert realized Sgt. Waters aim was to keep him away from Murringen until dark. His idea did not work. Walking into the kitchen and supply room billet, all was quiet as he called out. He walked into quite a scene. A Colonel and his staff (Inspector General) pointed to a pile of seven dirty and rusty rifles on the floor. They left with threats, with him not knowing what happened. The cooks and others scattered when he demanded to know how the rifles got there and no one made an attempt to clean them. An hour later, he answered a banging at the front door. Standing there weaving, were two large and drunken MPs. Between them was a petite nurse (Belgigue) wearing a white cap and blue cape. One MP said, "Say hello to the Sergeant." Smiling, she said, "Hallo, Sargahnt, you SOB !@!." He slammed the door in their laughing faces.   He guess she was being taught English.

The next morning about 0530, December 16, 1944, the Battle of the Bulge began.   The kitchen truck and supply trailer were loaded, waiting for the word to move out. Shelling was still heavy and also buzz bombs roared low overhead.   A driver with a ring mount machine gun opened up on one. Tracers arced into it and causeded it to about-face and later explode, hopefully at its origin. His division was attacked by five German divisions and it was murderous.   Bakers, cooks and every one were fighting.   He was a supply Sergeant, and the cooks, when the Germans were coming up the road, said they didn't have any ammunition.   He stopped an ammo truck to get them some.   A young shavetail lieutenant was kicking at him yelling "go go go" which was the right thing because the Germans were firing at them.   They asked for volunteers to stay behind with the wounded, a medical officer stayed and a couple of medics stayed with him, maybe one or two riflemen.   A month later when the area was re-taken they were found with their throats cut and bayoneted, they were all murdered.   This was the same area the Malmedy Massacre occurred.   A big fuss was made about the Malmedy Massacre of war prisoners. Many were attached to our division and It's been mentioned that 100/120 were lined up in a field.   The Germans backed a truck up to this field, opened the flap and machine gunned them.   One or two escaped.

After that incident there weren't many prisoners taken. The worst thing Albert saw was in the village of Murringen, his second battalion was lost for two days, He got out just in front of it. He was with the service groups getting out and he did see this, it might have been a Tiger tank. He was behind a building and the road coming up from the front made a right turn and he was behind a house looking around and there were wounded lying in the corner of the road and a German soldier was there waving the tank off around the wounded Americans. The tank turned and ran over the wounded and spun the treads grinding them into the ground in the snow and mud. That was the worst he saw. A couple kilometers beyond that he caught up with the whole group getting out of the area. Meanwhile his second battalion was surrounded. He reached this jam up at a cross roads, they were mulling about which direction to escape and he said that he thought Elsenborn was that way, some one had changed the signs. Planes were strafing, and down in the valley was a clump of woods a couple hundred yards away. Small arms fire was coming up from there. He had picked up an M1 and a Grease gun and was returning fire until the magazine ran out. They were just firing into the woods not knowing what they hit. So the Company Clerk and he left and headed for Elsenborn.

They found a log hut with smoke coming from a stove inside. They surprised the occupants; it was filled with sacks of potatoes, canned goods and hanging hams. The guys were down to their sleeveless undershirts. The stove was cherry red. Nobody spoke, as they backed out the door into the cold and hurried away. These "hut" guys had to be German Para's in captured GI summer undershirts. That cold night they found shelter in a shattered building.

Two days later the second battalion showed up. They came into Elsenborn starved, gaunt, without overcoats, tripods, mortar base plates. Many wounded. Many of the lost were KIA and POW's , later to be rescued by our division from camps. There was a ridge overlooking the bluffs and a plateau, it looked like it must have been a farm at one time. It was a large plateau with houses down in the valley and houses up to the plateau. To the North was camp Elsenborn. Our guys were immediately sent right out upon the ridge; They were in terrible shape. One good thing though that Major General Walter E. Lauer of the 99th Division had done, he didn't like our setup. We were covering right along the international highway 20 to 22 miles with our one division. We were hit by five Divisions. He didn't like the situation so he decided that he would have Elsenborn better defended. He had the Engineers dig fox holes so the guys had ready made foxholes made for them when they did come back. When Albert came back he saw three kitchen tent flies situated on this ridge so he went up to one, he smelled coffee, he hadn't eaten for about three days, and planes were coming over strafing. Our mess Sergeant was across this plateau and saw Albert. The Mess Sergeant was coming over and he yelled get "down, get down". The Sergeant took a head wound from one of the planes. Albert understood later from a V-mail letter here that the Mess Sergeant showed up back in the company area a couple of months later.

Moving on Albert ran into a little farmhouse. There were officers in the back room of this little farmhouse and they had let him in there to warm up, they had a cherry red stove going. Jasienski had brought stacks of mail that would go back to December 15th, so the stacks of mail were pretty hefty. It was too dark to try to sort any so he put them on a bay window. A German 88 shell came in wounding him in the chest and parked outside was a jeep belonging to Battalion, matter of fact, Sgt. Waters Jeep. A supply Sergeant from Battalion. It caught the jeep on fire; 50 caliber bullets were going off and naturally it blew in the window, started a fire and the mail sacks were burning. Albert was trying to eat for the first time in days, C rations, trying to start a fire out there in a stove. His back was hurt by the shell and he was lying on the floor when out of the wall, he thought he was in heaven because, white figures came out. What he didn't know, there was a doorway going up to a loft in this second floor farmhouse. The company clerk was up there and a dozen other guys. They were white with plaster. They were stepping on him and walking on him. Prior to the blast, Jasienski had him come out to identify two bodies on his jeep. Apparently one of those bodies was 39 year old W. Reppert, who had been told he could be discharged due to age, but wanted to go overseas with his boys; the other was a young lieutenant. (Forty five years later at a reunion in Pittsburgh Albert mentioned this to George Boehm the company clerk and he said that they were trying to put the fire out, they thought he was dead.) John Jasienski came out of the loft too. Jasienski never swore and never drank but he swore when he saw Albert's back. He picked Albert up and cradled him and dragged him over to the aid station where the medics were sleeping in the bakery ovens. Albert was going into shock. He could hear his voice saying "is there any medics in here", 'a voice said "who the hell do you thinks in here?" They gave him morphine and pinned a huge syringe on his collar and said they would put him in an oven. Albert kept saying "no! no! no!" So they put him under a butcher block table, then he passed out. When he woke up a few hours later, at day break, there was bombing, shelling and when he looked up he was under about a six hundred pound block on spindly legs. If it would have fallen on him it would have crushed him to death. An ambulance was backed up to the door and they got him up and put him on the ambulance. There was his friend Sgt. Waters, the one who lost the jeep, originally he had stolen the jeep and was changing the numbers on it.

They put him in the ambulance and it was riddled, just pock marked with holes all the way through. The only windows in the ambulance were little half moon windows in the back doors and it was pretty well lit up and up front he could see cowering figures, who the drivers said were Germans, about 13 years old who were killers though. A soldier got on with Albert and he took his bayonet and made gesturing motions and scared them worse. Albert told him to put it down. They took him a couple of miles back to a school house where they got hot cakes and coffee, he'll always remember that. A fellow introduced himself as a medic from Akron, Ohio, Albert Jacobs; Albert often wondered about him. He said he was a staff sergeant and wondered if he could have Albert's overcoat, it had a hole in it any way so he gave it to him.   The ambulance takes off down the road, suddenly some body was yelling and stopping the ambulance. It was one of the sergeant's superiors who ordered him to give the coat back. Shortly after that though, when he got back to Liege he was stripped of everything. Just prior to his getting wounded, Jasienski the jeep driver, came up with the jeep loaded with jackets, overcoats, drivers jackets, tankers jackets, overcoats from fellows in the rear, so they went down in the valley and up on the ridge, a stupid thing to do because he exposed the company Commanders Position. Just then one of the German spotters must have seen what was going on because they started to shell again. Then the Company Commander told him to get the heck out of there. Jasienski said he had these overcoats and the Commander said "Throw them on the ground and get out".

So from there on it was back to Liege, surgery and it got to be Christmas day when he came to and he was in a winterized tent. It had wooden sides and the cots were lined up back to back against the wall but in other areas they were lined up as they would have been in a barracks. He remembered a nurse saying, "Should it drain like that?" Then he'd go to sleep. About Christmas Day a fellow introduced himself and said that he was Private Jones from E Company, Albert was in G Company, Pvt. Jones must have known Albert, because he said his brother was a first sergeant and he would get him out of there pretty quick. He brought him a piece of fruit cake, he never drank before but he brought him a drink of sherry, schnaps, or whatever it was, and he drank it. Jones could hear a steam engine puffing pretty close, so he said," my brother said he would get you out of here back to Paris". So the next day, two German prisoners came in with a litter and put him on it and as they moved out of the door he could see the train down this walkway, kind of a black top walkway, snow everywhere, all of a sudden a German plane came over strafing and they jumped into one ditch and threw him into another ditch. They took him back and put him to bed in a cot. Some patients were killed, nurses killed, at the time they all had steel helmets on so he was in there another day until they got him on this train. The train was a blank car but they brought down side arms and set the litters on the arms. About this time he was feeling pretty good, he was still alive and getting out of there. A nurse was going up and down the aisle and suddenly he saw this little fellow who had his arms up in casts saying "I have to go to the bathroom". She ignored him and he said "hey nurse I have to go to the bathroom". She said," I just took you a little while ago" and he said "I have to go again". He was a Pilot, just a clown and he wanted her to take him to the bathroom. He jumped out of his fighter plane and the tail section must have broken his arms.

They traveled back to Paris in a convoy. They had 11,987 casualties in the battle of the Bulge. It was a constant flow. They were taken to this large general hospital in Paris that the Germans had occupied. He didn't know how many stories it was, but it was a huge building. The ambulances took them from the train to this hospital. They were there for a couple of days. The fellow next to him was in a hospital bed, the nurse was taking his clothes off and exclaimed, "you filthy thing I can't imagine anyone could be this dirty". Albert spoke up and he said "Lady he probably hasn't had a bath in four months." They didn't do any thing, they just put new dressing on him and a few days later another convoy took them to the airfield and flew them back to England. Albert wanted to be ambulatory and he said he could sit up. C-47 or DC-3 is the same type plane but what a glorious sight to see the white cliffs of Dover. He wondered if the plane was going to stay up because it was rattling. They landed at the airfield and there were low buildings all around that they put them in. Those that were ambulatory were put in the room on the second floor. All of a sudden he heard a commotion. A paratrooper had gone berserk and had a trench knife and was slicing people. They finally secured him.

Albert was placed in an ambulance and moved to another hospital, Albert didn't know if it was in Wales or just where it was. They did surgery on him there. He should have had a skin graft. At Liege they took the metal out of his chest, they entered the back and they stitched him up. When it spread apart it was transparent and you could see muscles and everything. He wondered where chow was and here the nurses were eating his chow and forcing him to go out in the snow with paper slippers to the mess hall. This went on for a few days and he rebelled and refused to go in that snow again. He was way in the back of this Quonset hut and there was this hospital Corpsman medicating somebody next to him and to this day he can't stand the smell of wintergreen or something like that. They were pouring it down the cast and finally they took him from there to a rehab hospital. At Exeter near Honnington England, it was strictly an Army base.

Fortunately he was given a job in charge of quarters and then they were shutting the camp down nearing the end of the war. He hadn't been paid in months and he had two weeks hospital leave. He borrowed four pounds from the Red Cross. A pound was valued at $2.80 American. For two weeks he was able to eat at various military places in London.

Then he had to report to Camp Litchfield. He didn't know where he was going from there. He heard of a Colonel Killian and that it was a treacherous place to be. There were about eight of them and he was carrying the paper work and he turned it in to headquarters. The staff said they didn't know what they were going to do with us. Albert asked why? "They said because they were filled". Meanwhile on a knoll going into this area, it was raining, it was in April and dismal weather, when he saw a G.I. chained to a stake in an open field by the drive as they came in. No cover whatsoever, it was rainy, cold. Albert heard about this Colonel Killian. He didn't know what this guy had done. He enquired of an M.P., "What has that fellow done", He said "Nothing, not much of anything". So fortunately they said that they couldn't keep them here so they put them in a house in the village with cots and blankets. Edward Edwards that he had met along the way was in their group; he had relatives in the town. His relatives gave them a hot plate, kerosene heater, coffee pot. One of the fellows would go up to the mess hall and come back with a few staples. But they lived with food they got in town; they got fish and chips and they stayed away from the camp.

The Army sent us back to France. They landed on V.E. day. The French people came out with bottles of wine, tomatoes, French bread and they were put into what was called 'The Cigarette Camp' for a few days. He was assigned to 6960 Repple Depot. Camped there for a few days where he was given a clothing warehouse. At Chateau Thierry, it was easy duty, they were billeted at the motor pool. This depot supplied a new nearby tent city called "Camp San Francisco". There were 10 of us G.I.'s, all recently discharged from hospitals in England. Each work day they drew 30 POW's from the stockade for a work detail. This warehouse had originally been a theater located on top of a hill on the road to Soisonnes. Italian prisoners had brought in timbers and constructed a second floor to hold additional bales of clothing. He was with a heck of a group. The motor pool tents had electric lights and some one would say turn out the lights or I'll shoot it out and bang, out would go the light. Finally the Army gave them a building in town and a half a dozen of them were billeted in this house. No furniture, but they had canvas cots and they had a home where they could go to get food from a facility that was staffed with German Prisoners. They could get their meals there. It was fairly decent duty but they begrudged the fact that every body else was going home. Headquarters asked if German prisoners were filling out requisitions, but I'm sure they knew this to be true when seeing the numeral "7" made by a German. Being only an hour drive from Chateau Thierry, Paris was accessible since we had a weapon carrier at our disposal. He had a blank pad of passes and if money wasn't short any three of their men could take a two day pass if they wanted. Lots of them stayed over for the Nurenberg trials. Many of the fellows from his division were actually in that court room. One of our men, Steve who was at Chateau

Thierry, that was famous for WW1 and Belleau Woods, was married and a little older than the rest of them. Each night he'd walk around the village and write letters home. One night somebody came busting in, saying that Steve had been picked up by the MP's for black market. They couldn't believe that, so they went to the police station where the MP's had him and he sent for this lieutenant Johnson. They wanted a lineup so they stood in the line up with Steve. The Frenchman picked out Lieutenant Johnson as the one who sold him cigarettes. They never did find out who it was, but it wasn't Steve. The 6960 Repl. Depot was disbanded in December, 1945.
.

Albert was discharged January 3rd, 1946 from Indiantown Gap, Pa

His ribbons and medals consisted of Purple Heart, 2 Bronze Stars, Combat Infantry Badge, European Defense and WW11 Victory Medal.

Albert and Miss Jane Bauer were married in January of 1946.

They have a daughter and one grandson.

He took advantage of the GI Bill, and took a two year course at Akron Law School, a traffic transportation course.

He worked four years for the ACY Railroad then to General Tire (Gen Corp)
in the traffic department. His practice took him before the ICC in Washington. He retired after 28 years, in 1980.

During my time in Europe, my closest friends were, 1st Sgt. Buzinski, Sgt. Waters of Battalion and George Boehm the Company Clerk. Buzinski and Waters receive battlefield commissions and George Boehm got my job.

His position at time of discharge was supply sergeant (MOS 821) line company.

Albert and his buddies, all from the 99th Division meet occasionally over lunch to hash over old times.

DAVID MICHAEL KUHARICH

David M. Kuharich, 15552 Stillwell Road, Huntsburg, Ohio 44046

He was born June 6, 1962 in Cleveland, Ohio

Graduated from Newbury, Ohio, High School in 1980.

He went from High School into the U.S. Navy, graduating in June and enlisting into the Navy and under the delayed entry program he reported for duty in September.

He entered boot camp at the Great Lakes Naval Station outside of Chicago, Illinois. He graduated from boot camp at the end of October. He was an Operation Specialist, radar, weapons, communications taught at

Damneck, Virginia, near Virginia Beach, that's where his aid school was. They taught gunners mates, operations specialists and some nuclear propulsions. He studied there about four to six months. From there he got orders to his ship and they were able to select where you went, according as to how you finished in your class. He was fifteen of twenty three, right in the middle, so he could have taken his ship which was in Mayport, Florida or to San Francisco. Deciding to stay closer to home he decided on Mayport. His ship wasn't yet commissioned so he was an original crew member, a plank owner. The ship was commissioned on June, 1981. When he arrived the ship had already been launched but the internal outfitting hadn't been completed. It was built and launched at Bath, Maine. When he got out of training he got with the members of his division and they were in Norfolk, Virginia for a while. They went for training and then returned to Damneck for FFG class 7 school. It basically taught you everything you need to know about the ship. Its operation the equipment that they would be operating and then to a fire fighting school. They then went to Bath, Maine and were stationed at the Naval Air Station at Brunswick, Maine, until their ship was ready. That was pretty neat because that was where all the P3 anti submarine big three engine prop planes were stationed. They would go out on twenty four hour flights up and down the coast looking for Soviet subs. He said that if you wanted to take a flight down to Florida for a week end to get out of the cold, you could get put on the manifest and you would be given a parachute and a place to sit. You would go out on patrol with them and they would fly all the way from Maine down to Florida but it took twenty four hours because they zig zagged around the ocean on the way. They would drop you off in Florida and then you would have to get back, either by flying back with them or arranging your own means. Dave went down there one time with them to pick up a car and as soon as he got there he had to rush back to get back in two days.

The ship was commissioned in June and they got under way and being a brand new ship, first they went to Philadelphia for a military day there and then they went to New York City pulling into the 42nd street pier. They spent a couple days in New York City and then to Fort Louderdale, Florida, from there to St Thomas then to Jacksonville, Florida at Mayport.

Mayport was their home port and once they got there they started training to get ready for their first Mediterranean cruise. They started out going to Guantanamo, Cuba for training and the reason they sent them there was because it was a hostile environment, the only American base on communist soil. He remembered that base pretty well, there was an air base on one side of the bay and the operations was on the other side. There were a lot of Marines there and mine fields, barbed wire so you had to watch where you went.

His ship the USS Flatley (FFG21) was only listed for 198 crew but they only carried 160. The only time they had 198 was when the air wing was aboard. The air wing consisted of two helicopters. Unless they were deployed they didn't have the helicopters. When independent steaming and by yourself training they didn't put a squadron aboard. When they moved over seas they included the air wing. It was a small ship and it was like a family and every body got along. They worked hard but they had a lot of fun. His ship was one of the highest rated in there squadron, they were in DESRON 8 which was Destroyer Squadron 8 which consisted of probably twenty frigates like the one he was on. The highest rated as far as readiness.

The ports he frequented were - Guantanamo Bay, Cuba, St Thomas, Martinique, Naples, Italy, Roda, Spain, Haifa, Israel, and one he couldn't remember the name of which was an operational base in the middle of no where. They called it the Rock. They also went to Roosevelt Roads, Puerto Rico where they did all their missile firing. They would launch drones off the island, either flying drones or remote control boats. He said that they weren't supposed to hit them but they did. They were just to come close but they shot down two drones and sunk a sub terminal so they were glad when they left.

When the Grenada invasion went down he knew about it two weeks before it happened. They were going to take part in that so they were briefed in it and given security clearance. The main reason for the Grenada affair was that the Cubans were building an airbase on Grenada which would allow the Russians and their long range bombers to have access to all of the United States. There was a medical school there and the students had to be removed and that was the excuse used to invade the island. They never had to participate but were held in readiness. The major concern was the Russian navy during the cold war. They would follow the Russian ships and the Russians would follow them – a cat and mouse game.

His ship was out for about five weeks and then they went to Guatanamo Bay and then over around Puerto Rico for a missile test. It was Halloween and they pulled into Roosevelt Roads and they just got off the ship on Halloween night so they went to the Petty Officers Club. There were a bunch of CB's and some Marines and waves and they were all dressed up in costumes and having a good time. His group was just in their fatigues, they just got off the ship and wanted to have a beer and something to eat. One of the CB's took a dislike to one of their cooks, a Filipino, and so the next thing he knew all hell broke loose. A major fight went on with chairs breaking, glass breaking and with all of them being arrested and taken back to their ship. They were made to leave so they ended up going to St Thomas setting there for a week. Dave was running across a street and suddenly his knee let loose. He tore his ACL. He had a lot of cartilage damage. His knee had suffered some damage during High School foot ball days and it was taken care of back then enough to get him into the Navy but it must have left some weakness that let go. He stayed aboard ship hoping that it would get better but it didn't so he turned in to the Doc who said that he would have to have it taken care of. When they got back to Jacksonville they sent him to the Air Station Hospital where the Orthopedic doctor said he had to have surgery. He spent the last fourteen months of his four year enlistment on limited duty. During that time he had two surgeries. His duties consisted in training fire fighting, leadership management training new petty officers and young officers on how to maneuver a ship. They did this through a big model pool where they learned to maneuver the scale models for docking, etc. It was a great duty, it was like having an eight hour a day job. There was about eleven of them on limited duty and they would help out where ever they could, in the class rooms, painting, maintenance on the grounds, driving, cleaning or what ever needed to be done. He lived on base but they didn't have enough room for all of them so they asked them to live off base. Dave got an apartment off base in Jacksonville right across the street from the University which was like a campus atmosphere which was great. Dave did take a couple of courses while there.

They had a program they called the Boost Program. Petty Officers that were interested in becoming Officers would be sent off to San Diego for a six months school to get you ready to go to college. They would send you to any college in the country that you chose that had an ROTC program. They would send you to college and when you graduated you would owe them another six years. Dave was interested and his Commanding Officer was very positive about it and said that he would write a letter to the Commander, the Admiral out of the Pacific, Fleet Command, and that was the direction that he was going when he blew his knee out, so that was it.

Dave said that he really enjoyed his time in the service and would highly recommend it to any body coming out of High School that wasn't quite sure what they wanted to do with their life. He said that he would highly recommend them into serving. Dave said that to him it was part of becoming a man, this is what you did, you went to high school, got out of high school, went into the service, went to college, got into a trade or whatever. He said that it was his idea of growing up. He said that he recommends it even with the troubles in the world today. He said that even if you ended up in harms way, still you come out of it such a better person than when you went in. It's worth the risk and the friendships you develop, the memories you have, it's all priceless. It molds you into a better person.

It makes you grow up because in the military you are given a lot of responsibility at an early age. There is no excuse when you are asked to do something you do it. You are told how they want it done and that's the way you do it, so you learn to take orders. Then once you've been in for a while you start to learn to give orders. It makes you grow up.

Dave said that some of the best people that he ever met or knew were in the military. They were fine people and no matter what they were involved in they were professional about it. He feels that this new group of Veterans coming home from the middle east will be adding greatly to our society. They are our future leaders, they know what sacrifice is, they know what team work is, camaraderie is, what service is. Dave said that to him you get more out of serving a greater thing than one self. He thinks that it's been lost with a lot of the young people today, they think of only serving oneself. There is nothing to be gained there, to serve something greater like your country or your Lord no matter what name you use is a great thing and you can't lose. He said that's what he got out of the Military.

Dave was discharged April 6, 1984. a little earlier because of his knee injury.

Dave married Denise Palumbo on June 8, 1996.

Some of his best service friends are, Ron Bentley, who made a career of it.
Ron Flefner, Tiffin, Ohio, Joe Lambert who spent thirty years in the Navy, Jack Colum, Boston, Mass., Scotty Waller, Houston, Texas.

PAUL EDMUND MACHUSICK

Paul E. Machusick, 12220 Lela Lane, Burton, Ohio 44021

Born September 21, 1943

Graduated from South High School graduating in 1962.

He enlisted in the U.S. Army National Guard of Ohio on October 4, 1964 in Cleveland, Ohio for a six year term. He was assigned to Troop A 1/107th Armored Cavalry where his Military Occupational Specialty became Tank Driver.
He started out in Headquarters Company.

Paul took his boot camp training and A.I.T. (Army Infantry Training) at Fort Knox, Kentucky. He served seventeen weeks at boot camp and at the rifle range scored Sharpshooter with the M1 rifle and Sharpshooter with the 45 Caliber Pistol. He had to crawl under the live fire and he said that he could remember they would be running and there were fox holes they would dive into. The man in front of him dove into this foxhole and it was full of muddy water so Paul just jumped over it and avoided jumping into any foxholes. He said that when he went in he weighed 170# and when he came out he weighed 140#.

He recalled that the platoons had inspections in the barracks and one Drill Inspector transferred out and was replaced by a colored Drill Instructor who was a Paratrooper. His Platoon came in last in the inspection and he ran his Platoon around the compound and each four laps was a mile. Paul said that he got tired of watching, they made so many laps. The Sergeant ran backwards every step of the way screaming at them all the time. Paul said that he ran at least five miles backwards screaming at them.

After boot camp they had meetings one weekend a month and field trips twice a year. They would sometimes go to the Ravenna Arsenal. One time one of the guys backed up either a tank or a personnel carrier and backed over a 57 Chevy and didn't even know it. It was an Army car and completely destroyed it. They would go there about twice a year for a week end. While there they would have training exercises with tanks, etc. Paul said that for a while he was a scout and he would be assigned a Jeep.

When with the tanks he was assigned as a bridge driver. It was a tank that had a folding hydraulic bridge on its top that would be driven into a ravine and the bridge would be opened hydraulically to form a bridge for the troops and vehicles to cross over. He said that he had the best job in the National Guard because they didn't have a bridge tank for him to operate. He said that he had that MOS for about three years. The one thing he liked is that he got to carry a 45 pistol instead of the M1.

The Armory that he worked out of was in Shaker Heights and was originally a tennis club that the National Guard took over. After he got out of the National Guard they moved the Armory somewhere else. When he was up for discharge they approached him to re-enlist which he emphatically declined.

Paul said that the first summer camp he went to they slept in pup tents. They had to dig a trench around it in case of rain and he still got wet. The next camp they brought along a four man tent with cots. As long as whatever you had was Army Green it was accepted.

During his time he was called out for the Hough riots, Lakeside riot, Teamsters strike and the Kent State University riot. He said that for the Kent State riot he was called up but stayed in reserve and didn't go to Kent. Teamsters strike was scary because they were standing by for the scab trucks to see that things didn't get out of hand. When the trucks came the teamsters threw rocks at the trucks and all the windows disappeared, windshields, side windows, etc. It was all over in seconds and then they got into their cars and left the scene. Another one was on Canal Road and Paul carried a M1 and when he went to load it the M1 was put together wrong and he had to field strip it and put it back together on location. At the Lakeside riots he was stationed in front of a store to help keep it from being looted. That was a rough riot because they had the police pinned down and one cop was shot and lying in the street. He said that there were four of them in front of the store and a short distance away was a group of young men about nineteen or twenty years old. They sent a little kid over to see if they had bullets and Paul said that he pulled the bolt down exposing a live shell and the kid went back and talked to the young men who turned and left the scene. If they had threatened them they would have been shot – that's what they were there for.

They went on maneuvers to Grayling Michigan a couple of times. Members of the communications would go up early to string up the wire and communication facilities.

They would take along a lot of food and drinks that they would bury in large 55 gallon drums packed with ice. They would have beer and steaks and what ever to go with them. Paul knew the guys from the pool room in his neighborhood and they would tell him to come over and eat with them. They would be grilling steaks and would offer him a beer which would be under straw buried in the ground with ice. At Grayling they ran around in tanks practicing war games.

One time they went to Virginia to fire the tanks and they had to go to NASA first where they were put on a National Guard flight. He said that he thought they were going to die because the plane was so beat up and uncomfortable. The insides were very narrow and the flight was rough, no frills. They got to Virginia and fired the tanks and flew back, a week end trip. They went to Kentucky for tank training and were firing machine guns at targets of old equipment, personnel carriers, old tanks, etc. They would shoot them up with machine guns and then they would shoot off the main gun but it would be at a target a way off in the distance. Paul decided that he would lower the gun down to see what would happen when he hit a more local target like the personnel carrier with a 105 mm gun. The tank commander lifted it up on him, he could override his actions. He knew what Paul was attempting to do. The 105's were loaded by hand one shell at a time with caution to make sure you were away from the recoil. Behind the weapon was a screen to protect the driver from the ejected shell casing. Paul said that he still had a scar from when a shell casing ricocheted around the screen and hit him on the shin.

Each year they went to Camp Perry in Sandusky for a weekend to fire their weapons. While there they bunked in old prisoner of war barracks.

At Fort Knox they were trained how to make some repairs to the tanks. They had a chain fall that was attached to the top of the turret to lift the breach from the howitzer for cleaning maintenance and repair. They would take the weapon breaching out clean it and clean the bore and replace it.

His enlistment was for six years which consisted of weekly meetings and two weeks each year at camp. The way it was set up you were afraid to miss any meetings because if you missed more than so many you were activated. The National Guard Units were only as good as the Commander in charge of the unit.

In the evenings they would play poker and one time when returning from camp in the back of a deuce and a half they were playing black jack and Paul said that he really didn't care for black jack but he played and when he got back he had so much money that when he folded it up he could hardly hold it in his fist. He won a bout five hundred dollars all in ones, fives and tens.

On October 20, 1966 he married Nancy Racky and ten years later November 20, 1976 they had one daughter Marilyn

He was awarded a Certificate of Merit, State of Ohio.

Paul received his discharge from the Ohio National Guard on October 3,1970., with rank of SP4, Corporal

Paul said that he thought his time in the National Guard was a good experience. He went in during the Vietnam War. Some of his friends was in the Army and didn't know if they would end up in Germany or Vietnam when some one suggested that they look into the National Guard. So Paul and a couple friends looked into it and decided that even though it meant a six year hitch they would enlist. He considered it a good experience.

EMANUEL MAGILAVY

Emanuel Magilavy, 3716 Wyndham Ridge Drive, #103, Stow, Ohio 44224

Born in Akron, Ohio December 17, 1919

Graduated from Central High School, Akron, Ohio 1937.

He joined the service at Patterson Air Force Base at Dayton, Ohio. September 21, 1941.

Parents were immigrants, father Daniel Isaac Magilavy from Russia and mother Idabell Kuttner from Austria/Hungary.

Parents had four sons in the service when his father died in 1943. A neighbor who was, at least formerly, a member of the Ku Klux Klan assisted his mother in maintaining the home.

He was already in the service when Pearl Harbor occurred. He was stationed at the Patterson Air Force Base and was in a transport outfit so he was aware of where Pearl Harbor was. Before Pear Harbor he had applied for flight training and had graduated as a flight officer which is actually a Warrant Officer. He had already picked four engine training and he was assigned to Sebring, Florida for B-17 transition. The training was fast paced but not made too difficult. He said that the instructors bent backwards to help you get through. He had already graduated flying school and it was one of the most thorough training schools that he had ever attended in the service. As pilots they were taught everything about that airplane – the B-17. The instructors knew their stuff and they went to different schools for different parts and different operations of the airplane. The flight instructors knew these airplanes thoroughly. He said it was the most interesting stays of any schools that he attended there. His attitude was that it felt like it was something that he had done all his life. The physical training part of it was rough but it taught you how to survive.

The planes that he had in training were PT17, BT13, BT15, AT6, AT9, AT10 and AT12. His favorite was the twin engine flying school plane that all students were required to check out in, the AT6. It was an airplane that he said seemed to him to be built around the pilot. When you sat in it you were part of it and it was part of you. The maneuvers and the airobatics you could do in that plane were just out of this world. He said that he enjoyed it more than he did the P17. The P17 was a plane that after you had soloed in it you could do practically anything in it. Comparing it with the AT6 it had more power and you were in a closed cockpit. It also had the advantages of radio and one time he had lost himself during maneuvers, doing something that he shouldn't have been doing. To find himself he used his link trainer experience tuning into a radio range that he was familiar with to find his was back to Albany.

It was noted that most pilots wanted to get into fighters but he wanted to get into bombers. He said that at that time he wanted to bomb Germany. Going through his training there were discussions on what was happening to the civilian personnel in Europe. He said that he had run into various Jewish boys in his flight training and when they had nothing to do occasionally they would discuss about that S.O.B. in Europe and how degrading it must be to capture civilians and treat them the way they did in camps. Usually their discussions revolved around flying first, then girls but they did get into politics occasionally.

It was noted that most Jewish officers in the Air Corp were either navigators or bombardiers. There weren't many pilots among the Jewish. He said that in Jackson Mississippi there was a boy named Silver and he had flown as a civilian and he taught his instructor, and the instructor admitted it, different maneuvers and he was very well thought of. Along the way he had met several that had washed out and it had never entered his mind that they had washed out because they were Jewish. In Jackson, Primary flight school, he was laid up almost two weeks in sick bay and instead of being washed out his instructor set him back a class. Originally he was in 43D and he explained that instead of washing him out he was giving him a chance in 43E. He said that he hadn't even soloed at that time and he really appreciated it.

Buddies in flight training with him were hard to maintain because they moved them around every two months but one was with him through advanced flying school and transition in Sebring, Florida and phase 3. He said that his Commanding Officer was Jewish. Captain Berkowitz the Commander of the group. He was respected as a pilot and a gentleman.

While in Albany and Augusta they were allowed off the base every other week end and he said that he had to admit that at that time he was quite a drinker. They would get into town with some of his class mates and would drink and fortunately they had a designated caretaker to make sure that they all got back to base. He and his room mate would take care of each other. Raymond Winkler from Memphis Tennessee. He was in a Berkowitz provisional group during training when they left Alexandria, Louisiana. They were in Pyote, Texas for first phase, Alexandria for second phase and third phase. He pulled out because he didn't want to go into combat and did some training in the states. When contacted after the war he said that he was ashamed to even contact him. He was ashamed because of what he had done when he was German and Emanuel was Jewish. That was the last contact.

Emanual said that as a Prisoner of War when he came back he didn't discuss any of his experiences even with his family. He said that he blocked it out and that he had nightmares galore. He threw his wife out of bed – he busted windows – the nightmares were horrible. He couldn't get any help at that time and it wasn't until 1982 when he found out there was a special physical for ex prisoners of war. By then there had been enough back ground to find out what was causing all these problems with the prisoners of war. It was through a neighbor who was also a prisoner of war that introduced him to the fact and encouraged him to go there saying that it had done him a world of good.

The physical that he was given at the V.A. installation, in one part of it they went with a psychiatrist and a psychologist and one doctor there got things out of him that he had never spoken about to anybody. When he realized that he had said it, she was a very sharp person who talked to him and got everything out of him. Since that time his nightmares have diminished and he is able to talk about almost anything that happened.

He was sent to Sebring, Florida but he wasn't assigned to any group as yet. At Sebring he trained as a pilot. A B17 Pilot. When he left Sebring he went to Pyote, Texas where they formed their crews. At that time they were still in transition, it was things training, he referred to it that way. They had three phases of training before combat. First he was brought up with his Co-Pilot, Joe Hayes. Then they got several of the enlisted crew and did some training under the second air force. From Pyote they went to Alexandria, Louisiana to the Alexandria Air Base. Here they were assigned a navigator, Peter J. O'toole, and they had a bombardier, a Captain that had gone through Bombardier training as an officer. He said that he didn't get that acquainted with him to find out if he had washed out as a Pilot or whether he had gone in to be a Bombardier. They lost him due to the provisional group training ahead of them had their Bombardier taken away from them and sent directly to England. So he was moved to fill in that group. That is when they acquired Harvey Greenfield in Alexandria.
Then they had their complete crew. That's when Berkowitz went with them to Kearney, Nebraska. That is where they picked up an airplane to fly across to England. From Kearney, Nebraska they pre flighted

their plane to check it all out. They flew to Presque Isle, Maine and stayed there until the weather was clear enough to continue on to Goose Bay, Labrador. From Goose Bay, Labrador they flew across the Atlantic to Valley, Wales. The B17's were scheduled for different destinations and theirs just happened to be Wales. The plane that they flew to Wales wasn't the plane that they flew in combat. That plane they took to a depot, where modifications where made for combat. From the depot they took the train to this replacement center. From there they were assigned to the 96th. That was between Christmas and New Years in 1943, as a complete crew they were assigned that way. That's when they got assigned to the 96 Bomb Group, 413th Bomb Squadron.

His crew when they were shot down on February 10th,1944 was the crew that came with him from the states. They were coming back from their ninth mission. Previous to flying with the crew in their first mission, most pilots and co-pilots were sent as observers with other crews. The flight that he was on the pilot had to abort because of mechanical trouble. The Co-pilot had one more flight in than the rest of the crew. In the crew Peter J. O'toole and Joe Hayes were his closest friends. Joe Hayes and he had worked so close as pilot and co-pilot. The Pilot and Co-pilot didn't tend to socialize with the crew on the base but when they got into town and they would run into some of the crew it was different. Once on the plane it was a completely different story. On the plane he was known as Mac

And Joe was Joe and on the plane that was what the crew was to call them if there was something that came up that they needed to talk to one of them. Their quota of missions at the time was twenty five. On the first five missions he had two or three different airplanes, then on the sixth mission they were assigned their own airplane a new B17. They never did get a chance to formerly name the plane but one of the crew members came up with the name Discovery and it ended up in the 96 history book. They acquired a deep affection for their aircraft

And he said that they were always looking for something to hang on to. It was like their lucky piece or a charm. He said that a plane to him was constant, it was real. He said that you could loose a crew member in a hurry but felt like the plane was constant, but you could loose a plane to, which they did. He said that it was what got them there and got them back, something they could hang on to, like a symbol of permanence. He said that like a lot of others he felt like it wasn't going to happen to me. He said that for eight missions it didn't and when it did happen he said it was like a daze. He did kind of expect it and when it happened he knew exactly what to do. They didn't discuss it but they did practice for bail out. That was routine. In flight he wore a flack jacket and there was extra armor plate under his seat.

The tail gunner and the ball turret operator accounted for hits on German fighters.

He said that the B17 was the only four engine plane that he ever flew and he always referred to it as a truck. Demand decisions were required and you always had time in case of an emergency. Once he had a trainee co-pilot who had been a B26 pilot and during some maneuvers he seen him reaching for controls and he would motion him not to touch it. When they got back on the ground the co-pilot explained to him that in the B26 anything that happened like what had happened to them on this flight he did what he did immediately and didn't sit back. Emanuel explained to him that in all of his hours in the B17 you always had time to sit back before you made a maneuver.

The living conditions at the base were in huts, before they were adorned with inside insulation. They had one pot belied stove and they had three or four crews sharing each hut. It consisted of one large room filled with cots. In their free time he mostly read, made one trip into London. They had all squadron sessions in which they were briefed on maneuvers, etc.

He said that at Sebring, Florida, Avon Park American Air Force Landing Depot he had flown the earlier model of the B17B which he claimed was a horrible air plane. He also had several flights in a B17C, B17D mainly they had the B17E's in Sebring, Florida.

While in training in the states he at tended Jewish religious services at Dayton and he kind of remembered

Alexandria, Louisiana. He said that very strange to say they had Jewish services in the prison camp. He said that a boy by the name of Hank Levine, from Syracuse, had trained to become a Rabbi, then gave up and went into law. Hank got permission for them to hold services every Saturday and they would go in, he had some one make a Mogen David for him. It was in the early part of 1944 and their barracks Commander in the prison camp was also Jewish by the name of Margolin. Emanuel went every Saturday until they got transferred out. All the Jewish boys were transferred into one barracks. There were quite a few and Hank conducted all the services for them. Hank taught himself Russian and when the Russians liberated them he became the official interpreter for them. Hank was a navigator and had gone to school with Emanuel's navigator. There were at least one hundred and fifty Jewish boys in the camp. Some because they weren't detected didn't become a part of the Jewish camp. Some that weren't detected would attend church services. One that he remembered was Sammy Fogel who attended a sunrise Easter service. He was a gymnast. He said that also there was a Frank Kapeles from the Bronx that was in his room. Also a Stanley Silverman from Cleveland, Ohio.

Emanuel said that one of the persons that he had met at one of the P.O.W. conventions, by the name of Gregg Hatton who is writing a book about his fathers experiences. He has been interviewing ex P.O.W.'s for years. He believes that Hattons father was Jewish and one incident when his father was transferring, his father was on one of those marches, and they came into Stalag-1, a new barracks, when supposedly a guard came in and wanted the Jewish boy that was in there requesting that he step forward. All the men stepped forward.

Emanuel said that in his south compound there was a section for British. He said 'What a sense of humor'.

Emanuel said that he and his crew never discussed any concern about their flights through flack and fighters. They just wondered why it didn't hit them. Once you flew through it, it was gone. The fighter attacks that they had before the last day was so minute as they went by that only one member of the crew had a chance to shoot at them. Other pilots that they talked to said it was the same way until the day that they got shot down. Some of them said that they hadn't even seen a fighter. He said that the day he was shot down unfortunately they had to make two passes over the target. They lost an engine the first pass and lost a second engine the second pass. Emanuel said that with one engine out you could keep up with the formation but when he lost the second they became a sitting duck. That is when you attract all the fighters.

When comparing the B17 to the B24 he said that he thanked his lucky stars that he was assigned the B17. He said that he saw too many horrible explosions of the B24. He said that he saw a horrible one when they were assembling on a mission. He said that it was a B24 that ran off the runway with a full load of gas and a full load of bombs, a one great big ball of fire. During his time in the prison camp he saw B24's blown apart by fighters. This was in the fall of 1944 when the deep penetrations were being made into Poland. They would be flying over their camp. They would be forced to go back into their barracks and they would raise hell, yelling for them to bomb the hell out of them. He said that in his mind the B17 was a better plane because it took more punishment. The B24 had more hydraulics making it vulnerable to having lines severed and subject to more fires.

On the particular mission that he was shot down he said that they got hit the minute they hit the coast of Europe. It was fighting all the way into the target. Both flack and fighters. Up until the target naturally it is to avoid as much of the flack area as possible. When in the flack area you are not under the bombardment of fighters because they don't want to get hit with flack either. The target area of Brunswick that day seemed like a blanket of flack. He recalled the first time going over and the fact that they didn't drop bombs and making a three hundred and sixty degree turn in the flack area. He said that the squadron lost three airplanes that day. He said that all he thought of was keeping the airplane in control. The Pilot is in radio contact with the squadron, the Co-Pilot is gunnery commander and he is in contact with the rest of the crew. If required he would tap him on the shoulder and point to the position on the command set which only the Co-Pilot and he could talk back and forth. Aboard ship each position of the crew fought a different war, something he became aware of many years later. Emanuel said that he had a tremendous guilt complex being the Pilot, the Commander, losing your command, losing your ship. It left him incapable of discussing it with any one and he didn't contact the crew and they didn't contact him. When they finally did get together he learned things that he didn't know about. Each position had their own conditions that they were concerned about. Emanuel said that now they are quite close and there are only six of them left. Up until the last day the flack and fighters didn't bother them. The engines that were out were on opposite sides of the plane with the last one on the Co-Pilots side. They were on fire so they had to bail out. All of the controls had been shot away and he had set the automatic pilot and he thought it was taking hold but he wasn't sure. The Co-Pilot tapped him on the shoulder warning him that they were on fire. A rocket was imbedded in the wing and was on fire so that was when they all decided that they better leave. They were between Brunswick and Hanover when they bailed out. They were on the way back and left the target area. They were over German countryside and when they bailed out they were over twenty thousand feet altitude. He said that he executed a delayed jump and it was the only jump he had ever made and it was terrific as far as he was concerned. He was without an oxygen bottle and he knew that he had to get down lower. He was also aware that he had to be on his back before he pulled the ripcord to avoid the cords to rip across his face and he did exactly that. It was cloudy and he couldn't see any other chutes and very cold. He said that he realized that the war was over for him.

He said that he landed in a field and for some reason he was trying to save his parachute. The wind was dragging him across the field and when he realized where he was he stood up and ran across and collapsed the chute. He buried it in a ditch and after he had it covered he knew what direction that he wanted to go. He knew he wasn't very far from a little village. He started off to the road and he saw a school bus coming and it unloaded. The children got off and they made a big circle around him. They didn't get too close to him but no matter which way he would move they would move. When he realized that for him it was over he just sat down. A man with a Tyrolian hat on and a little pistol came walking down and all he could say was that he was his prisoner. He acknowledged that and they wanted the chute. Coming from a home where they spoke Jewish he could understand a little German. So he understood that they wanted the parachute but he kept shaking his head so they drew a diagram that showed that they wanted the parachute. One little girl pointed to where he had buried it and they uncovered it and attempted to make him carry it but he was kind of knocked out, shook up from what had happened , so a couple of little children carried it. They took him into this village and took him into a house and the women grabbed the chute, and it was gone. One woman came out and took his hand and took him into the kitchen and opened up the stove and had him sit down next to it. There was a maid in there that had a Star of David band on her arm. The man that brought him in was the head man, or the Mayor, and one woman when he came into the kitchen she pushed him out. She said leave him alone that she wanted to give him something to eat. They sliced him some bread, that he eventually learned to like, but he couldn't stomach it then. Ersats bread and Ersats coffee that he couldn't drink and a little later a fellow came in who was limping and he could understand that he was a German fighter pilot that had been shot down. He asked Emanuel if he was a fighter pilot or a bomber pilot and he just stared at him and he lifted up one finger, two fingers, then four fingers that ment how many engines. He noted four engines. He stayed there until a bus came by with some of his other crew members. The German people were very kind to them. What tee'd him off was it was a Ford V8 buss. It took them to an Army camp. It was to a Wermacht Camp someplace. They were interrogated but he couldn't tell if it was with an officer or an enlisted man. He asked the interrogator about his Co-Pilot and he was told that he understood there was one man in the sick bay. He allowed him to go over to see him and the Co-Pilot had a fighter shell go through his ankle. The only thing that held his foot on beside his boot was a sliver of his Achilles cord. Joe Hayes spent almost all of his prisoner of war times in hospitals. They treated him fine. They were then taken by bus to some gathering point where he met more members of the crew and wound up in Oldenburg. That's where they started in box cars, 40 & 8, and he doesn't remember how many days they were in those box cars. It was a lot of Americans, not only him and his crew. They were taken to Frankfort, the interrogation center. He spent six day in solitary confinement, counting the cracks in the floor, the nails in the walls. He said that the interrogator told him more than what he was asked. The interrogator knew all the flight schools that he attended in the states, he knew when he graduated, he knew that he flew to Presque Isle but he did not know whether they took a boat or they flew and he wouldn't answer him. He felt that this guy knew more about him than anybody else. Personally he knew that he had a relation in Oil City, Pennsylvania by the name of Mogilowitz. The Germans had files on everybody. One thing that Emanuel asked him was about his crew and he said that they had all of them. He knew that he was lying because one man was killed in the air. He showed him pictures of his hard stand, where his airplane was parked, in England. He knew the missions that his crew flew so he knew that somebody had to talk. When he got back with his crew they had all been told the same thing and they had all felt that somebody in the crew had blabbed. That wasn't the case. None were subjected to brutal treatment.

After Frankfort they were sent to a transient camp and stayed there until they were shipped to a permanent camp. From Frankfort they were shipped by box car again to a camp in Germany. He didn't see the crew again until March. O'Toole was there, he was in a different compound. Harvey was in the same compound with O'Toole. O'Toole was quite a politician and was made librarian and he was able to visit other compounds to exchange books. Harvey he didn't see again until all the Jewish boys were moved into the one barracks. The different compounds couldn't intermingle with each other.

During his free time to keep from going batty he did, as he said, a hell of a lot of reading. He read through the Old Testament and he used to discuss a lot of questions that he had with Hank Levine. He said that he read it about two thirds of the way through. He said that at one time he even went to the Catholic Padre. He was asking him questions until the Padre found out that he didn't want to convert. Then he didn't have time for him. They did have classes so you didn't loose interest. Many sessions where you would sit and talk for hours, with your room mate. Paul Teetor was an interesting crew member. He was a professor from New Jersey and they would usually use him as their final authority. If you made a statement you better be able to back it up. Rumor mongers – they had rumor committees and if a rumor came before them they attempted to trace it down. He said that at one time he kept a diary of all the books that he had read but in all his movements it was lost. He was interested in ancient history and as much as he could get on that he would get. They received a lot of paper backs that came through from the International Red Cross.

He said that before they were segregated his bunk mate was Jim Bridges from Brevard, North Carolina. Another that he happened to meet again just recently was a man by the name of Robert Warner living in Dayton, Ohio. He met several of his room mates in Las Vegas three of four years ago. Ray Argast was one of them. Gerald Hanus was from Milwaukee and was installed with him as the first two in their room. There were twenty men in their room. Their discussions revolved around flying and women. The first or second religious service that they had they introduced themselves to each other. One boy asked him if he was from Akron and when he told him his name he asked him if he knew the Magilvy's. He informed the boy that they were his cousins. The boy said 'I married your cousin.' Nathan Waldman from Detroit. He had been shot down and was with the underground for quite a while. They held their services on Saturday mornings. They would take down the crucifixes and put up the Star of David and replace everything before they left.

Emanual said that he talked to Hank Levine and the Catholic Chaplain about these questions concerning where it stated why they were against inter marriage in their religion He said that he had married out of his religion and it prayed on his mind quite a bit.

They became segregated in January 1945. Jacobs came around and told them he had been given instructions that they were to be packed and that they would move out the following morning. The next day they moved into the Jewish barracks which was in the North Compound. The new barracks were better than the ones they were in. He and Frank Karpeles had discussed escaping but they knew that they had better talk to Margolin. Margolin said don't do anything because everything will be taken care of. They were told originally that they were to be taken out of that camp to a concentration camp. He heard that their Commanding Officer, Zemke had interceded and had made a deal with the German Commanding Officer that the Jewish boys would not leave the camp and would be moved into a compound by themselves. They were moved to a barracks in the North Compound and that is where they stayed until the Russians liberated them. Zemke would assure the German Commander that he and his family would be given safe passage to Sweden once they were liberated. After the Russians did liberate them they saw the German Commander with his wife and they assumed it was his children pulling their cart towards the bay. They heard all kinds of stories and one in particular was that Zemke had threatened the German Commander stating that he had eight thousand men under his command with no guns and that he only had three hundred. He said that maybe he would loose several thousand of his men but the German would loose his command if he tried to move the Jewish boys off the camp.

Emanuel said that when the Russians liberated them that Hank Levine was immediately grabbed up to be their interpreter. Many nights they would have to carry Hank back because they wouldn't let him get away without drinking. Hank got together with some of the Jewish Russian officers and they set up a Friday night dinner in his room and in their room. The Russians brought in tables and white table clothes and he said that he didn't know where they got it but it looked like Salad. They brought in wine and Vodka and in their room nobody understood Russian but they sat down and started eating and drinking and before you knew it you were holding conversations with them. He said that you understood them and they understood you. The Russian boy setting beside Emanuel was saying how much he wanted to get home and back to his farm get married and raise a family. He told him what he had been through where he had started and each room in the camp had a map depicting what was happening with both allies during the war. He pointed out where he had been in Russian and how he had ended up there. He said that they had a wonderful time. They socialized with them. Just one night. He said that he remembered the Russians coming in and they wondered why they still had fences around them. He said that they were told that they had to tear down all the fences around the compounds and that they were to wear black armbands. The black armbands was because of Roosevelts death.   Emanuel said that one Russian truck driver grabbed him to show him his truck, it was a Dodge. He showed him every bullet hole in it and he knew it came from America and what a great truck it was. He got up into his truck and got them some orange juice and a Russian officer came by and he had to stop.   Other prisoners said that they had also been grabbed by Russian truck drivers who where so proud of their trucks.

Emanuel said that while they were prisoners they were allowed one time in the summer of 1944 to go swimming in the Baltic.   Each compound, each barracks, at a different time.   The city of Barth he had seen coming through from the train but he didn't see it when leaving because they were flown out.

As a Prisoner of War the hardest thing was the restriction. The being confined behind barbed wire and not being able to walk out and freely walk around. Not having access to a comfortable lounge chair or something with a back on it to sit down and stretch out and be comfortable. Also the food

It was rumored that the Russians wanted to hold on to the Prisoners and to be marched back through Odessa for repatriation.   Zemke stopped that by getting in touch with the British/American allies and got word through command that they weren't to be moved out. It was Zemke's doing.   Then they were flown out in B17's to

Camp Lucky Strike, France. He got reunited with the tail gunner and crew chief there. Cliff Speare was the turret gunner and Lloyd Gray was the tail gunner. They came to his tent at Lucky Strike, they were the only two. He flew back to England to the base and to London and left Portsmouth on an LST to the States. They landed someplace in New Jersey and then he was sent up to Fort Hamilton. Next he went to Camp Attlebury, Indiana then to San Antonio, Texas and from there to Sioux City, Iowa. Hank Levine joined him in San Antonio and Emanuel's wife and daughter drove their car to see him so that he drove to Sioux City then on to Akron, Ohio where Hank spent some time and then went back home. Emanuel had some emotional conflicts as to whether to stay in the service but he didn't want to stay in as an Officer. He would have liked to have stayed in as a Flying Sergeant because of the freedom and he found out he could stay in but would loose his pilots rating. So he decided he would get out and as a flight officer he didn't have to be in the reserves. He received his discharge January 11, 1946.

When the war was declared over in August 1945 he was driving down the main street in Akron, Ohio with his wife and daughter.

Emanuel married Billie Van Dyke December 7, 1942. Emanuel said that his war started one year after Pearl Harbor. They had two daughters and two sons.

He and his son own a dry cleaning operation in Akron, Ohio and he just retired in 2004..   .

.Emanuel said that his opinion of the Veterans Administration was that personally, they had saved his life.   When it was discovered that he had prostrate problems he was put into the V.A. Clinic in Cleveland, Wade Park facility.   When the facility became the subject of a 20/20 program he said that he blew his stack because of the inaccuracies of the program.

He said that he had a doctor that was very concerned about a blood condition that he didn't like.   The V.A. didn't have the facility to give the proper blood exam that he needed so he was sent to a hematologist at the University Hospitals in Cleveland and when talking with him for about a half hour they were quite sure they knew what his problem was. He is one of five children in his family and it was decided that he had a condition that occurs with Jewish parents, when both are Jewish. It's the factor eleven blood deficiency.   His V.A. doctor wasn't aware of this condition and if he had gone ahead and operated on him for the Prostrate problem the surgery wouldn't have been prepared for what would have happened to him.   It required that he be prepared with plasma and whole blood before surgery and same after surgery.   He remained in the hospital for two months.   He questioned whether a civilian hospital would have done for him what this hospital did for him. So when he hears people condemn the V.A. Hospitals and doctors he becomes upset because he still has medical, dental and physical care in the V.A. Hospitals and their facilities.

He keeps close contact with remaining crew members such as Cavanaugh and Harvey..

His citations and decorations consist of European Theater Service Medal, American Theater Service Medal, American Defense Service Medal, Air Medal, Good Conduct Medal, Purple Heart, P.O.W. Medal, Victory Medal and the Ruptured Duck Lapel Button.

He's a member of the Veterans of Foreign Wars and the Ex Prisoners of Wars.

DANIEL MICHAEL McDERMOTT

Daniel M. McDermott, 14957 Sperry Road, Novelty, Ohio 44072

Born January 25, 1924 in Cleveland, Ohio

Graduated from Shaker Heights High School in 1942

Enlisted in the U. S. Navy in October 23, 1942 and served his boot camp at Great Lakes Navel Station, Camp Green Bay, and went to school for pharmacy there. Some aptitude tests were given and as a result Dan and a Chuck McCullough were chosen to become Pharmacists. It wasn't exactly what he would have chosen but decided not to make waves. Then he was sent to the Pensacola Air Force Base. That was where he was introduced to the Southern prejudices. He was in Pensacola and waiting at a bus stop and there was an elderly black lady with a bag of groceries in each arm. They were waiting at the same bus stop so when the bus came along and stopped he told her to go ahead. The bus driver screamed at him 'do not let that nigger to go in ahead of you'. He said that he had never heard anything like that before and never has since.

He was at Pensacola for two months for additional training and then was sent to San Francisco Bay Area, Treasure Island. He went aboard the S.S. Matsonia and shipped out to Numeau, New Caledonia. He was there two months awaiting another ship. He then went aboard the Del Brazil for transport to Guadalcanal. Every one said it was an old banana boat and it was surely a scow. When you got up in the morning and got in line for chow by the time you got to the mess hall it was closed. They would run out of food. Some of them would volunteer for KP (Kitchen Police) to insure they got fed. They would steal canned food out of the storage compartment. They were only served two meals a day. When they would go by the crews quarters they would see them eating gourmet meals. He said that he remembered one night when they had spaghetti and there were pretty rough seas this night. He came out of the mess hall which was down between decks and the hatches were covered with canvas with a metal band around it. He had his tray of spaghetti, a slice of bread and a cup of coffee when he hit the metal and the ship lurched and the tray went up in the air. Some of the guys were sitting there when the spaghetti flew up into the air making them look like they were decorated for Christmas. They didn't think it was funny. When it landed he caught the slice of bread and that was all he had to eat for dinner.

They disembarked on Guadalcanal then went aboard APC 35. It was a ship constructed of oak wood. He was told that the shipyard, at San Diego, was a builder of tuna ships. He said that the ship had an eleven foot draft, twenty three foot beam and was one hundred thirty foot long. It could attain a speed of about fifteen knots. It maintained a crew of three officers and twenty three crew members. His duty as a Pharmacist Mate was always aboard small vessels for medical service. The APC stood for a troop transport coastal. They traveled to the Russell Islands up to New Georgia. They would join small convoys.

On September 23, 1943 they were traveling through Renard Sound, New Georgia when heavy seas struck them. Although there compass showed that they were on course the heavy seas was forcing the ship to the western side of the channel. The ship struck a reef tearing a fatal hole in the hull well below the water line. The ship could not be moved from the area so they couldn't beach it. When abandon was called all hands dutifully and sadly left the ship with commission pennant still flying but the U.S. colors retrieved. They abandoned ship on their one whale boat. Dan and another enlisted man volunteered to return to the ship to gather and destroy all material documents and maps. The wardroom was completely emptied of all items of need and bagged into sea bags and removed from the ship for destruction. They had to walk in water up to their shoulders in which diesel oil was floating. They both suffered from fuel oil burns over the major portion of their bodies. They abandoned ship at 1:30 AM. Luckily they suffered no loss or injury to personnel.

The U.S.S. Pawnee a sea going tug passed them during their fatal hours and received their distress signal but they lacked IFF radar. She continued on her course but did come the next day and picked them up. They were aboard the Pawnee for about a week. They went to an LST that had been strafed and a bomb had gone straight up from the bow to the stern and it was an abandoned ship. The Pawnee had to go along side that and being temporary crew this other fellow and he had to go aboard the LST and clear the decks. He has always felt bad about that because they were instructed to just toss the bodies they encountered over board without removing their dog tags. They just couldn't take time out to pull the dog tags. They had to toss about twelve to fifteen over the side. Then the Pawnee towed it back down. He thought that he would be able to jerk the tags off the bodies but they were burned pretty bad and the chains wouldn't break. Fortunately they didn't have to go down below decks to clear out bodies and he heard that there were about ten or twelve bodies that were just incinerated.

They went back to the Russell Islands where he was assigned to LCI (L) 65 a troop carrying vessel. Later they were converted to a gunboat LCI (G) 65. When they went from a troop carrier to a gunboat the crew increased from 23 enlisted men to 65 with three officers. Prior to his assignment to the LCI the ship had suffered a near miss and had a hole blown in her side. She went into dry-dock for repair. The hole was about 10 x 12 feet right in the area of the quarters where he bunked out. He was the only one in the room that was 23'x25'. The gunboat was fully outfitted with weapons like 20mm, 40mm sticking up any place that there was room and a 5-inch cannon on the forward deck. The LCI had loading and unloading ramps on each side of the bow, but when they converted to a gun boat they removed the ramps and replaced them with rockets. Dan said that he didn't know what happened to the LCI 65 after he was transferred but he did hear that it took a bit of a hit on one of the early trips into a battle zone. Dan said that they would go to the Russell Islands two or three times but they would only be there one or two weeks then they would be gone somewhere. The LCI's were basically landing craft infantry and had a shallow draft of three feet forward and five and a half aft.

Dan said that an interesting thing about the men that were assigned to the gunboat were from the Mare Island Naval Prison. They had a choice to serve their time, go aboard the landing craft gun boat as hazardous duty. He said that was a real moral builder. Some were real hard cases and others weren't to bad.

Before the ship was converted they use to handle troops and go up to the New Georgia Islands quite frequently which was a disbursement base. While they were in a convoy they would be trolling for fish and they would get tuna, baricuda, etc. The tuna they kept and ate and the baricuda they would give to other crafts who would request food from them. One of the boats that came along side was PT 105 that was captained by a future president. They use to come alongside to request food and water.

When converted to a gunboat he remembered on landing on an Island that he only knew as Treasury Island, but was never able to confirm the name. It was a stepping stone on the way to Peleliu. They traveled down along a channel into a bay a bout three o'clock in the morning on idle and they passed Japanese gun emplacements so close that they could hear them conversing as they passed. Come daylight they were well within the bay and they landed troops and before noon they had it all secure. It was softened up by battleships and cruisers down range from them firing over their heads before the troops landed. The projectiles going over head were an awesome sight. Army soldiers went in to mop up and one group finished up to fast, they weren't expected until about eleven or eleven thirty and they finished around ten and when they appeared back at the beach it caused some exciting moments because they were taken as the enemy. Some got hurt. It was well executed.

On another occasion one of their ships in the convoy got hung up. There were a lot of reefs and mostly uncharted and this one got hung up and were trying to back it off. One of the cables that was attached snapped and hit the Captain of the ship in the back throwing him forward to the deck. They had these one inch treads welded to the deck and the Captains head hit them. They had to have some one volunteer to go over and treat him because they didn't have any medical persons aboard. Dan being the only one on his ship he volunteered and a coxswain took him over. It was rough seas that caused them to get hung up in the first place. He treated him and then went back. The Captain was removed and he did survive. The Captain was moaning and groaning and had strictly head injuries. With head injuries you aren't supposed to give morphine but with this pain he felt that he had to do something so he opted to give him a half dose of one of the tubes of morphine. Hopefully that it wouldn't do what it could do and applied methiolate to the wound. He also marked the Captains forehead with an "M" for morphine. He was later informed that he had done the right thing.

From the LCI gunboat Dan got sent back to Guadalcanal to the Fleet Hospital #108 for three or four months then sent back to the states. He went back on the USS Sea

Hawk, a liberty ship and served as temporary duty. He was assigned to six soldiers and they used the old brig because they were mental patients. He had to see to their care, taking showers, etc. Battle fatigue displayed itself in various ways, mostly non violent, but required attention. Some confirm thought of suicide. One claimed to be a golfer and invited Dan to play a game with him. He did some time later but decided that it wasn't his game.

He landed back in San Francisco to Treasure Island and later on January 18, 1946 he was discharged at Shoemaker, California. Shoemaker was an area near Sacramento. They wanted to send him back to Great Lakes for discharge but he wanted to visit some one so they allowed him to stay for discharge in California. Then a troop train ride back to Cleveland.

Dan married Ann Ostanek on January 14, 1950.

They have two daughters.

Under the G.I. Bill he went to Cleveland College but was disenchanted with how they conducted there courses so he didn't complete it for a degree. After that he took other courses on his own.

His medals consist of American Area Victory Ribbon, Asiatic-Pacific with two stars and the Good Conduct Medal.

He was discharged as a Pharmacist Mate Second Class.

His attitude toward the service was good, he had a lot of experiences and seen a lot of the world.

Lately Dan has been diagnosed with lung cancer for which he is being treated. The doctors in attempting to diagnose the source of his ailment discounted smoking but in questioning him about asbestos Dan remembered that the LCI 65 had taken a near miss before he had been assigned to it and in his quarters, where he slept, they had taken it over to dry dock and they had torn out all this insulation and left some exposed. It was considered that it was where he had been exposed to asbestos.

CHARLES RHODY MELIUS

Charles (Chuck) R. Melius, 1754 – 25 Ave. No., St Petersburg, Florida 33713

Born in Bedford County, Pennsylvania on January 23, 1943, a dark winter night at the Howard Kinton Ranch. Actually just a large farm house in the countryside where his parents worked as farm hand and cook.

After going to school at Snake Spring Elementary then graduating from Bedford High School in 1960 at the age of 17 he enlisted in the Navy. On August 15th he entered boot camp at the Great Lakes Naval Training Center in Illinois. After spending 9 weeks living in dilapidated facilities from the 40's in hot miserable conditions, including catching measles and spending several days in the infirmary he managed to graduate.

From there he carried his duffel bag across the marching fields to enter the Hospital Corps School nearby where he spent six months taking courses in nursing and field medical training to become a Hospital Corpsman. One of the major reasons that he chose to be a Corpsman was because his oldest brother, Melvin Cruthers, a Marine in WWII in the South Pacific, had told him how a Corpsman saved his life when one of his legs was blown off during combat.

Upon completion of training in April 1961 where He learned much about the medical profession he was sent for duty to the Chelsea Navy Hospital near Boston, Mass. He worked in their surgical ward taking care of sick and injured service men and retirees. It wasn't exactly the hardest duty to have but there were times when seeing and caring for the men and their conditions could be heart breaking.

After applying for more training he was sent to Portsmouth, Virginia in late 1961 for another nine months medical training as a pharmacy technician. This was a very intense school and took much study and hard work to complete. He graduated in 1962 and was sent to the Navy Department Headquarters in Washington D.C. in the dispensary pharmacy where he spent the remainder of his Navy career working and filling prescriptions written by the Doctors on site. Our patients at this facility ran the gamut from active duty seamen to retired Admirals. During this time John F. Kennedy was president and some of the Corpsmen would go to the White House to take care of the people there in Kennedy's staff including Kennedy. He didn't do that but he did fill prescriptions for Kennedy and family at the Pharmacy in the Naval Dispensary where he worked and also for President Johnson and his family after Kennedy was assassinated.

Much was learned from working in such a facility, however one late Saturday night while on Emergency Room Duty he was sent on an ambulance run to southeast DC where a young serviceman's wife was having a baby. Apparently she was early with her pregnancy and at the time they were having a party for her at their apartment. The party guests were still hanging around with drinks in hand. There he found her on the living room couch with the baby just born on her stomach and the husband trying to do what he could. With the help of his ambulance driver they got her on a guerney into the ambulance then drove to the nearest medical facility they could find. As he sat with her in the back of the ambulance tying off the umbilical cord and making sure the baby's eyes were clear and medicated he thought how thorough his training had been to know what to do in a situation like this, especially since it came from a military school.

From that time on his only thoughts were to leave the Navy and to find training in some other field of endeavor which he finally did. He became a telephone company installer and technician and retired in 1995 with some 30 years service.

You see he is a Gay man. Though he was able to be sexually inactive while in the Navy, he also was unable to live a life free as other men. This kept him from staying in and making it a full Navy career. Not exactly your common military story this one, but an honorable one.

He received an Honorable Discharge January 2, 1964

He received a Good Conduct Medal.

Rank at time of discharge was HM3 (E-4)

STEVEN NEMCIK

Steven Nemcik, P. O. Box 154, 15503 Auburn Road, Newbury, Ohio 44065.

Steven was born August 1, 1922 in Czechoslovakia.

Steven came to the United States as an American Citizen. His father was an American Citizen and his mother was from Czechoslovakia. The way it started it was right before 1938 the Chief of Police came to the house over there and told his mother, "You know Ama you're not an American Citizen and you're kids are American Citizens so if you don't send them back to America they will end up in a concentration camp." He advised her to get in touch with her husband and make preparations to go to the USA otherwise they are going to take the children away from her and she will be all alone. So she wrote to her husband and he got them Visa's and Passports and brought them to the U.S. Other than that they would have probably died over there. Hitler hated Americans, his Gestapo came into the same town that Steve lived in and killed off all the Jews. The Gestapo took them out into a field and shot them. His dad was from Cleveland originally and that is where he was living and working. In 1933 he was in the United States for one year. He came back to the United States in `1938 at the age of 15 ½ , straight to Cleveland, Ohio.

Kissinger came here at the same time he did in 1938 and became the number two man in the country. Kissinger still has an accent and he noted that he doesn't have an accent. He said that he can no longer speak the language but he does understand it. He still has aunts and uncles over there.

He graduated from John Hay High School, Cleveland, Ohio. He went to St. Francis graduating from there and then went to John Hay.

He enlisted into the Navy October 17, 1942 and did his boot training at the Great Lakes Naval Station.

He had commercial training before he went into the service so they gave him all kinds of office jobs right there.

His first assignment was Fargo Bldg. YMS Pool for duty in Boston, Mass. Where he recorded personnel assigned to various ships. From there he went to the commissioning of USS Intensity in Quebec, Canada. We put that ship in commission right there in Quebec and sailed out on the St Lawrence River to the Halifax and they operated from Halifax for a while, North Atlantic patrols, anti sub, that ship never carried any bottom so if a sub would attack it, it would have to hit it on the surface and in the exact position in order to scuttle it. Most of the time a torpedo would go under the ship.

After that we took the ship out to sea for another six months. Went to Boston and that's when the ship was turned over to the Coast Guard. The Coast Guard took the ship to the Mediterranean somewhere. From Boston he went to Portland, Maine Navel Station and from there he went to Brunswick, Maine Navel Air Force. He had various assignments over there. From Brunswick he went back to Pier 91, New York and from New York he went to Woods Hale, Mass. He was assigned to the Narragansett sea frontier. It was some kind of specialized unit but he still did office work. From there he went to Nantucket, R.I. Navel Air Station. From the Navel Air Station he went to Woods Hale, Mass. Navel Station. From there he went back to Nantucket. From Nantucket he went to the Newport R.I. Navel Station. He was attached to the war college. Special assignment taking notes on war games that were conducted in Casco Bay. From there, Pre Normandy invasion, at Casco Bay he was on a sea going tug. Taking notes on all the activities of the ships that were to be sailing in what direction, in what groups and the U.S. Tuscaloosa that was in charge of the Atlantic Fleet under the command of Capt. Jones. The tugs were pulling the targets, floating targets that would go twelve miles beyond the horizon and the ships would charge them to see how close they could get to the targets. That's when he went to the Portland, Ma. Navel Station, staying there for seven or eight months. Then he was sent to San Diego, Ca. and waited for further assignment. Then he was sent to San Pedro where he shipped out on the USS Orestes AGP10. That was an AGP tender. The USS Orestes got hit just before he boarded it and they lost 67 men from a Kamikaze attack. He never experienced conflict himself. If it had hit the torpedo room, the ship carried torpedoes to load them on the PT Boats, stacks and stacks of torpedoes and if they had hit the ship there—goodby ship forever. The sailors use to tap them for alcohol, 200 percent alcohol in them, but fortunately they never had an accident. The men came from all over from every walk of life and in short order they were handling the ship in perfect order. He said that some of the guys that he met in the service were brilliant. He said that aboard ship it was sometimes scary and the port holes were all blackened but he was always with the Commanding Officer at the top, at the Helm, so he would see every thing. Some time they would be way up high one minute and the next all you could see was mountains of water. North Atlantic was much worse then the Pacific. When he was aboard the USS Orestes he ran the ships office. He was preparing complement transfers and a lot of personnel work.

He sailed down to the Philippines, Solomon Islands, Taiwan, Sumatra and the base was at Ulithi. From Ulithi they use to repair the PT Boats. They were attached to the PT outfit there. From there they were headed towards Tokyo Bay after about several months, it was in August, 1945 and the war ended. Then they were rerouted to Manila. From Manila he transferred to another AGP Tender, the USS Acontius, AGP12, and after being anchored there for four more months, something like that, we scuttled the PT Boats. They were all tied in a circle and we set them on fire. They were made of plywood and that was it. They went to Leyte in Mindanao and picked up about three hundred soldiers and shipped them back to San Francisco. Then he stayed on the Acontius until they decommissioned it at Hunters Point in San Francisco. Then he stayed in San Francisco for three more months till all the paper work and everything was taken care of. Then he was sent to San Diego and from there returned via train to Great Lakes, US Navy Personnel Separation Center Unit #3. He was discharged April 25, 1946.

From Great Lakes he came back to Cleveland, Ohio.

When he got back he went to John Carroll University for a couple of years. He married Mary Ann Varady in 1948.

They have four children, three girls and a boy. They have four grandchildren.

He worked for New York Central, Chesapeake & Ohio, Baltimore & Ohio then to Fisher Body General Motors where he retired in 1982.

He has addresses of some of his contacts in the service but he doesn't communicate with any of them. At one time he was invited to a reunion of the USS Orestes at Kansas City but he didn't attend.

In the service he had it made when it came to living quarters. He said that he served as a court reporter because he could do short hand. It was for Court Martials, etc. One guy a Chief Petty Officer committed sodomy on a kid after the war was over. They tried him and they left him off the ship in the Philippines where the Navy took over. He was fortunate to have some very good jobs. At one location the Commanding Officer near an air station, would take the Captains gig and go to the hospital there and pick up a nurse for himself and they brought her over moonlighting on the top deck. The Commanding Officer was from Chicago and he owned a trucking company.

His rating at time of discharge was Yeoman First Class.

HARRY PLISEVICH

Harry Plisevich , 15355 Munn Road, Newbury, Ohio 44065

Born in Cleveland, Ohio December 18, 1922

Graduated from East Tech High School January 30, 1942

Enlisted into the Airborne December 11, 1942 through Fort Hayes, Ohio

Boot camp at Camp McCall, Georgia

He took his advanced training at the Parachute School at Fort Benning, Georgia

On January 18,1944 he embarked for Europe from Camp Miles Standish in Boston, Mass.

Statement made that he really wasn't a very religious man but for a long time after the war he wouldn't even step on an ant. He went out of his way to keep from killing any creature.

One of the closest contacts he made in the service was Leonard Morris from West Virginia. They went on Maneuvers in South Carolina one time and he acquired a bag of pears. Six guys proceeded to take them from him and he ended up in a fight. His friend Morris noticed that he was fighting with six guys so he came over and they each took on three. They were dukeing it out pretty good when someone hollered MP's was coming. They backed off and mingled within the crowd acting innocent.

He became attached to the 101st Airborne Division. On D Day, June 6th, 1944 they were to parachute behind the German lines in Normandy. They were not aware that the Germans with the thought of stopping the allies advance from the rear had flooded the area behind their lines. They landed in the flooded area and he became detached from his unit and was lost for a week behind enemy lines. He hid in hedge rows sometimes in ditches wading in water up to his chest to avoid the enemy. An American tank came along and he managed to get back to the front lines. Fortunately for them the plane they parachuted from never made it back to base. It was shot down some time after their release.

In December,1944 they were loaded into trucks and moved to the Village of Bastogne. The Lieutenant sent him and a couple others to scout ahead to check out the enemy's strength. The Germans had closed the gap and had Bastogne completely surrounded. Instead of the Germans holding their positions they made a mistake and instead of pursuing their advantage, they backed off. He said that they were down to very little ammunition and they wouldn't have been able to hold them off long. American tanks moved in and helped them to escape.

Later he was chosen to check out other areas patrolling way out front. The Medic was acting as a runner. He reported to a Captain that they were being over run by German tanks, but the Captain said there weren't any tanks in the area and he was commanded to return to his position. On the way he made a wrong turn and ran into the German Army and was captured. Plisevich's patrol was also captured and they were made prisoners of war. They were forced to move out and one of the prisoners had been hurt so they made a skid so that they could drag him with them. He found that his Lieutenant and the Medic runner had also been captured. He will never forget the look in the eyes of a Belgium lady that befriended them, offering them something warm to drink. The prisoners were put on a train in boxcars called 40 & 8, forty prisoners and eight horses. They were locked in and he said that they would look through cracks and noticed the beautiful landscape they were traveling through. The train was attacked by American planes so they drove into a tunnel and hid. Later they moved out and soon the planes showed up again and started strafing them. One of the prisoners came up with a bright idea and they were allowed out of the boxcars and ran into a field where they formed their bodies into the letters POW. The American planes circled the area for a while but discontinued shooting and then left.

The German guards decided to continue on foot but they didn't get far. The American POW's were using some pretty bad words and not being very cooperative. The Germans kept prodding them to go faster because they knew our Army was coming. General Patton's Army was coming fast and soon overtook them then came back and cleaned up the area. General Patton marched right through the area and liberated them.

He was then sent to France where he got back together with Leonard Morris.

He was given an opportunity to place a telephone call home and when his mother answered and he said "Hi Mom" she wanted to know who this was. After all he had been declared missing in action twice. It was a very traumatic experience for her.

Shortly after he was freed, March 28th he wrote the following letter home –

Dearest Mom and Pop:

I'm so happy, and everything is so nice that I don't know where to start. I sent you a cablegram and hope that you all didn't worry too much. Everyone is treating us wonderfully and I'm so thankful, thankful for everything. First naturally for being liberated, then food, and everything you wouldn't give a second thought to.

I don't know if you were informed that I was a prisoner of war or not. So much has happened that I don't know what to write. After I was captured I was sent to a hospital to work. They treated me well and there was no kick about the food, but then I was sent to a P.O.W. camp where things changed.

The Germans tried to evacuate the camp and sent us deep into Germany, but because of the push of the Allies and the Air corps we were forced to abandon the railway and walk. We moved slowly (despite the guards forcing us to hurry: because some were sick and wounded.) Then the armor caught up with us and the guards fled, because we refused to move further and our dreams and prayers came true – we were liberated.

I'm sure I can't ever come near expressing how thankful I was to God for everything. We were all bubbling over with joy and happiness.

After all were liberated we ate, and I mean good ole lovely K rations and some Red Cross parcels. I sat down and opened everything, throwing all caution to the wind, because I wanted to get gloriously sick from eating.

We were treated like human beings again and whisked back to a hospital. I just had a bath that money couldn't buy and not only that – but got deloused. Aside from aching all over, I'm fine and in good health – minus 35 pounds, but as I get the stomach back to normal I'll get it all back plus.

Mom, I assure you that you will find me a much better son than when I left home, much more appreciative of everything. I've had plenty of time to think, I've prayed often and I know that it was God who has been watching over me and answered my prayers. Perhaps you people have been praying too. I'm sure you have. All I know is that I'm ever so thankful, more than words can say.

God bless you all,
Your loving son, Harry

He was discharged December 12, 1945 with the rank of Sergeant in Parachute Infantry from the Percy Jones Hospital Center, Ft. Custer, Michigan.

His medals consisted of – Combat Infantry Badge, Victory Ribbon, European African Middle Eastern Theatre Ribbon with three bronze Campaign Stars, Good Conduct Medal, Purple Heart, Bronze Star Medal and the Distinguished Unit Badge, American Theatre Ribbon.

He received his Purple Heart from shrapnel wounds received in Belgium on January 3rd, 1945

Citation for the Bronze Star Medal

Corporal Harry Plisevich, 15377623, Parachute Infantry, United States Army, for heroic achievement in action. On 16 June 1944, the company of which Corporal Plisevich was an assistant squad leader, had the mission of pushing back a strong enemy road block. His platoon, the assault platoon of the company, was pinned down by heavy enemy machine gun, mortar, and artillery fire from commanding ground. Corporal Plisevich voluntarily crawled forward approximately 45 yards, although exposed to enemy observation and heavy automatic weapons fire, and located a position from which he could employ his rifle grenade against enemy machine gun positions. His action forced the machine guns which had pinned down his platoon to withdraw making it possible for his company to disengage without suffering heavy casualties. His actions were in accordance with the highest standards of the military service. Entered military service from Ohio.

Signed by – Richard D. Bush, Capt., FA AGF Liaison Officer.

He was married to his long time sweetheart Miss Constance Rose Intihar on August 17, 1946 in Covington, KY.

His family consists of a girl and a boy. Linda and Harry,Jr.

He retired on May 31, 1985 from Lucas Aerospace.

Service buddies – Leanord Morris, West Virginia
                  George King, West Virginia - deceased

OTTIS H. PORTER

Ottis H. Porter, 12558 Jackson St., Burton, Ohio 44021

Ottis was Born November 8, 1923, Route# 3, Franklin Co., Russellville, Alabama.

He was raised on a farm where he worked as a farm hand on his father's farm, Franklin County, Alabama, prior to induction in the army. He plowed, planted and cultivated crops of cotton, corn, hay and garden vegetables. Used a team to plow and cultivate the soil. He tended to the livestock, and the poultry, while performing the usual farm chores. He also helped to keep the farm tools, building and fences in good repair.

He was drafted on January 1,1943 and went to Fort McClellan, Alabama for his physical Then to Fort McPherson, Georgia for his induction before being sent to St. Louis, Missouri, Jefferson Barracks for his boot training. He was there until April when he was sent to Venice, Florida for advanced training. While there he was given very casual firing of the M1 and 50 caliber machine gun. They brought a team of regular Army down from Alaska to form a new outfit which was the 1877 Aviation Engineers that he remained with during his whole stint in the Army. During his boot training it was all done with wooden rifles. His advanced training was in Mechanics and Parts.

From there he was sent to Patrick Henry, Virginia where he embarked for overseas duty. While at Patrick Henry they were there for a couple of weeks and he got the job of hauling garbage. When they assigned KP duty they would take a whole company at a time. There were thousands of men there waiting to ship out. They got him for KP and he went in there and he liked to do pots and pans better than anything. He and another guy got there pots and pans all washed up by about nine o'clock and they were tired. You had to get up about four o'clock in the morning to get ready to serve breakfast. They got it all cleaned up and went and got a shower and crawled up into their bunk. About the time he got into his bunk he heard a racket and every one was running out the door. He wondered what was going on when the Sargent came through gathering up guys for KP. He figured he was safe because he had just gotten off and he wouldn't bother with him. He said your on KP tonight. He said he had just got off KP but the Sargent said he was the only one available. So he got his clothes on and went over there and reported. They had a little guy that was a KP pusher who said they had six stoves here and six stoves over there and they wanted to bake tonight and they wanted them hot. He said that they were as hot as they will ever be if they are waiting for him to fire them. The other guy had been on KP that day and they were standing talking. They looked up and here come a Colonel with the Mess Sargent. He said it's going to hit the fan now. He just stood there and never moved. The KP pusher went over and was talking to the Mess Sargent and they were looking over his way and he thought it's either do or die. They called him over and they said, you been on KP to day and he said yes sir. He asked for a list they had showing who was on KP. The Colonel said check the list and see if he was on KP today and they said yes sir he was. The colonel asked if they sent him over to do double duty and he said yes sir that he had just got off KP and they sent him back over. The Colonel said get that Sargent on the phone and it wasn't five minutes before someone was there to replace him and the Sargent came with him. He said he didn't know what they had told him but the Sargent never bothered him any more.

While there they had Italian prisoners held there. He got duty driving a garbage truck which the Italian Prisoners would gather and he would haul and unload. He went over on a British ship that served very lousy food and they disembarked at Casablanca on Christmas day 1943. From Casablanca they went to Iran, via a cattle train, then on to Algiers and arriving in India in February. While in India they built an airfield, the first B-29 Base at Chiculia,India before moving on to Burma. They were convoyed across India to an airfield where they dismantled there trucks so they could be flown with them to Burma.

His summary of military occupations consisted of – Mechanic, Engine Wheel Vehicle – was assigned to the 1877th Engineer Aviation Battalion, with service in North Africa, India and Burma. He served as a mechanic, in the Battalion Motor Pool, repairing and adjusting vehicle motors. He disassembled motors, ground valves, installed rings, pins, bearing, rods, etc. Rebuilt and adjusted carburetors, clutches, brake systems and fuel pumps. He replaced starters and generators, when necessary. He also replaced worn and damaged rear ends, transmissions and universals. Used all types of mechanics hand tools, and testing equipment, to locate and make repairs to motors.

Automotive Parts Clerk - Worked in the Battalion Parts Section, issuing, receiving and storing automotive parts and accessories. Filled requisitions, and issued parts to the mechanics as they would order. He also picked up parts for stock at the Quartermaster Depot, which were brought to parts section, for sorting and storage in their proper bins or racks. Kept a record on the bin cards, of the quantities removed from, or replaced in stock. He helped to take periodic inventories of stock on hand. He drove a 2 ½ ton truck in conjunction with the above duties.

To get some of the trucks and heavy equipment up to the Burma road they had to cut them in two. They would dismantle the wiring harnesses and drive shafts and upon receiving them in Burma would reassemble them. He claimed that they had very few problems with the reassembled equipment. They did have problems acquiring all parts they needed which required a considerable amount of ingenuity on the mechanics part. The much heavier equipment such as road graders, rollers and cranes, etc. was flown by C-47 airplanes. The large trucks were held till the road became passable and driven in.

Their job was to carve a supply route 270 miles long through very mountainous territory from India to China. His outfits duties was to build bridges. He remembered being strafed by Japanese planes once but our pilots put a stop to that. They all jumped into there foxholes but the pilot concentrated on the headquarters tent. The only damage noted was he shot a hole through the Commanders air mattress. There were three airfields in Burma which was used by fighter planes, supply planes and personnel movement. They built one of the airfields for B-29 traffic. They were built along the Airwati river. He said that a lot of the work was done by natives. The men would do the digging then they would lift heavy baskets of dirt up and the women would step under them and walk off with them on there heads to wherever they would dump them. The women wore dresses that crossed over there shoulder and exposed one breast. One day a soldier reached out and grabbed one of the woman's breast. All of the women immediately dumped there loads and walked off the job. It created quite a problem for those in charge and they had a very difficult time to encourage the women to continue working. There was an endless line of them revolving around with there loads picking up and dumping. Needless to say a meeting was held with all about there conduct.

They suffered with insects, malarial mosquitoes and typhus. The animal population consisted of tigers, elephants, snakes, mule deer and a variety of other critters. Like in India the cattle was considered sacred and roamed freely. His unit lost two men, one was accidental shot by the belly gun of a B-29 that was discharged by accident and the other from typhus.

The terrain was very mountainous with one mountain there that was nine miles long. The mountain was so steep that trucks would role backwards when changing gears. Land slides were a constant threat. It was a supply route from China through Burma to India and as soon as it opened the Chinese flowed through there like water. The road was 270 miles long and it would take you all day to travel it. You had to put on chains to travel it because of the hills road base and mud. There was a colored unit of truck drivers that had been there for 30 months and he said they were the best drivers he had ever seen. They traveled the mountains like on level ground. The trucks all had governors on them but he was sure that the colored drivers had found a way to do away with them because they would pass them up like they were standing still. He said that many men lost there lives on the road. He didn't know exactly how many but they used to say how many men per mile.

As with most services food was a problem but the cook assured them that there was enough cows running around that they would be able to get enough beef. Of course the cows was sacred and any beef better be kept quite. They had a place where they would pick up eggs from a native which helped. Ottis and several of his buddies went on a hunting expedition once and they came across a nice stream. One of the guys produced a couple of sticks of tnt which was the promise of fish. They threw them into a couple of holes which made quite an explosion and soon fish started to surface. They removed their clothes and jumped into the river and gathered all the fish. The camp enjoyed a good fish dinner that day.

After Burma they went back to India where they stayed for about three weeks waiting for transportation out. They flew to Karachi where they shipped out for home.

If they had of taken a train to Karachi it would have taken them seven days, but flying out took them eight hours and twenty five minutes. They flew in a C-54. They stayed in Karachi three or four weeks before they shipped out around the first of December, 1945 scheduled to arrive in New York the first of January, 1946.. They arrived, due to a storm, January third. They sent them over to Camp Kilmer, New Jersey and the next day they started sending them all home. He was loaded on a train to Fort McPherson, Georgia and was discharged January 7th, 1946. He was on his way home. When he was discharged he was a T-5 (Corporal) ranking.

One of his closest buddies was Emery Whiter from Alabama. Another one he used to talk to occasionally was Bascomb, from Cleveland. He hasn't kept in touch with any one.

In April of 1946 he went to Cleveland, Ohio where he met and married Pauline Isbell. They were married 52 years when she died of a prolonged illness. During his marriage he moved around quite a lot, Leesburg, Bushnell, Orlando and a couple of other places. He returned to Alabama for a short while then to New Mexico for a part of a year then back to Alabama, finally returning to Cleveland in 1948.

They had three children, two girls and a boy.

He took advantage of the G.I. bill studying Mechanics and Body Shop.

He went to work for Chevrolet Motors until his particular division shut down in 1962 when he was transferred to Terex in Hudson, Ohio. On May 30th, 1980 he retired after 30 years.

Recently he remarried, Jane Gichenko and they have settled down to a happy married life.

DONALD ALLEN SCHUTT

Donald A. Schutt, 14899 Caves Road, Novelty, Ohio 44072

Born November 13, 1930 Cleveland, Ohio

Attended Chester High School and received his GED under the Veterans preference in 2002..

Enlisted in the U.S. Marine Corp. October 1st, 1948 at Chesterland, Ohio

Attended boot camp at Paris, Island where he received all his basic training then was shipped out to Treasure Island, California. From there he was sent to Guam. In Guam he joined the 5th Marines line company. He was attached to the Motor Pool and served on Guam for just over twenty eight months. He served on Guam from February 3rd, 1949 to June 8th, 1951. His position there was Motor Vehicle Dispatcher. While in Guam he experienced one of the South Pacific typhoons. There were winds of 172 miles per hour with torrents of rain and lightening. He still has some pictures of the devastation to the facilities there. His motor pool activities became quite demanding after that for a while.

On Guam he was located at Camp Witek where his responsibilities consisted in dispatching motor pool units to service the needs over the Island. On Guam they still had Japanese prisoners in a stockade. There were still a few Japanese hanging out in the hills and would sneak down occasionally to pilfer what they could. On June 1st, 1951 he crossed the International Date Line, 180th Meridian, and after being duly initiated was accepted into the Domain of the Golden Dragon. He is now a member of the Domain and can cross the International Date Line at will without further question.

After Guam he returned to the states landing at Treasure Island the 21st of June and then flew from there to Los Angeles, laid over for a day, then flew to Chicago. He then flew home to Cleveland where he was on leave for thirty days. He then went back to Quantico. He was a Buck Sergeant and while there he was promoted to Staff Sergeant. He spent the next fourteen months working out of the motor pool at Quantico. He received his discharge August 15th, 1952. They wanted him to re-up and promised him a raise of rank to Tech Sergeant but he declined it. He said that he wanted to see what the rest of the world looked like. He said it was a learning experience and he put a lot of values on the Marine Corp.

When he got home he was offered a trade through George A. Rutherford Co. assured that whatever trade he chose they would get him into the Union. He took up his dads trade as a carpenter and he would have to spend six months as an apprentice. He got home on August 15th and he started work on August 18th. He was accepted into the Union immediately. They took him to NACA (today it is NASA) it was the starting of the propulsion lab putting in the main drive and secondary drive bases. That was when Jet engines were just being started. After that he worked in various plants and buildings around the city. While he was apprenticing he went under the G.I. Bill to a trade school learning his chosen trade. It was a four year program. He got a Diploma from Cleveland Public Schools as a Carpenter Apprentice.

He was married November 22, 1953 to Margaret Clifford from Russell, Ohio

They have three children, two boys and a girl.

His awards consisted of the Good Conduct Medal.

Some of the comrades he is still in contact with is – Roy Foor, Erie, PA.

Harry Fontana, Chicago, IL.

Richard Siciliana, Burton,OH
He had some CB friends, Gene Painter, Chardon, OH, Dick Dryer Russell, OH and Francis Abfall Orwell, OH. They get together at the senior center on Thursdays for breakfast. A chance to reminisce with their service time memories.

HARRY H. SHIRE

Harry H. Shire, 248 Steele Ave., Ashland, Ohio 44805-4311

Born September 12, 1920 in Ashland, Ohio

Graduated from Ashland High School 1939

He was drafted July 6, 1942 and entered service July 20, 1942 through Fort Hayes, Columbus, Ohio

His boot camp training was at Camp Crowder, Missouri. They got them all together there and they called out names and said you were going into training here or there. He ended up in the last batch of maybe twenty a part of which was sent to Springfield, Ohio and the rest including Harry was sent to Indo, California. His opinion of Indo wasn't very good but that is where he ended up in Radio School. He actually started his radio training in Missouri but continued in California. Then he was sent to Arizona where he did sending and receiving of Morse code. While in Arizona the movie Sahara was filmed and they used their location and equipment. Then down to Fort Polk and then to New York for Embarkation out of U.S. Camp Shanks on March 31st, 1944.

He landed April 8th, 1944 in Scotland but wasn't there very long until he was sent to England to Hampton Park where he received some advanced training in communications to become a High Speed Intercept Operator. Their equipment was considered inferior so they were using German intercept material. Upon completion they were told that they were in highly secret interception and if they were ever captured they had the option of committing suicide or suffering torture by the Germans to extricate information and then being killed. A no win situation.

That's where he became attached to the 3256 Signal Service Co. of the 69th Signal Battalion, 20th Corp, 3rd Army. They would position him in a location where he would search radio bands for German transmissions. He would record whatever he heard and forward to Army Intelligence who would translate. He would record the Morse code but would never know what the translation was. They had direction finders and cryptographic people. They intercepted and recorded day in and day out but they were never allowed to transmit anything.

Due to his position he saw very little action, but one time a group of them were told to go and take two Germans prisoners that were spotted in a barn. So they went and demanded that they surrender when some one noticed a rifle barrel being extended through a hay loft door. They all raked the area with rifle fire and it ended up that four Germans were killed and a number of Germans came out of the barn with a white surrender flag. They got 32 prisoners from the barn. He didn't know if he was responsible for any of the deaths.

Years ago while it was still fresh in his memory Harry Shire wrote the following record –

The Ghost Corps, 20th Corp
Of General Patton's Third Army

From the day the twentieth corps landed in France until the end of Hositlities at Rieds, Austria, this Corps was destined to become one of the greatest fighting units in history.

The drive of the 20th Corps started with the break through at Avranches, France. The drive of the 20th Corps from St. Jacques to Verdun France, 600 miles in 30 days was one of the fastest sustained marches in history. In this drive alone General Walkers 20th Corps crossed six rivers, The Loir, Seine, Vesle, Marne, Aisne and the Meuse.

Some of the towns and villages that fell to the 20th Corps in 1944 were:

Fleury	-Aug. 4th
St. Martin De Londolet	-Aug. 5th
Vitre	-Aug. 7th
Soulge De Briant	-Aug. 10th
Le Ferte Bernard	-Aug. 13th
Courville	-Aug. 15th
Chartres	-Aug. 17th
Dysonville	-Aug. 22nd
Milly	-Aug. 23rd
Fontainbleu	-Aug. 25th
Donna Marie	-Aug. 27th
Jutigny	-Aug. 28th
Montmirail	-Aug. 28th
Louvots	-Aug. 29th
Ville-En-Selve	-Sept. 1st
Ste. Menshould	-Sept. 1st
Baleicourt	-Sept. 2nd
Verdun	-Sept. 2nd.

600 miles in 30 days – next to fall were:

	Voinville	-
Sept. 8th		
	Mars-La-Tour	-
Sept. 8th		
	Jurny	-Sept.
24th		
	Thionville	-
Nov. 20th		

At this point most units were out of gas, tires were in bad shape, and all supplies were very low. On November 9th began the attack on Metz. This was 20th Corps most costly battle. Metz fell on the 22nd of November.

In December the battle of the Bulge began. The same units that fought at Metz were sent into the Bulge. The 90th Infantry Division, 5th Infantry Division, and the 10th Armored Division.

On February 19, 1945 the drive into Germany.........

The Moselle-Saar Triangle was cleared. The towns of Thron, Kazen, and Wiltingen fell after heavy fighting. Trier fell on March 2nd. Some of the towns and villages that fell in Germany were:

	Trassem	-Mar.
16th		
	Saarburg	-Mar.
20th		
	St. Wendel	-Mar.
20th		
	Kaiserlautern	-Mar
21st		
	Kirchheim-Bolanden	-
Mar. 23rd		
	Ober-olm	-Mar.
26th		
	Weirhof	-Mar.
30th		
	Wiesbaden	-Mar.
31st		
	Alsfeld	-
Apr. 1st		
	Falkenburg	-
Apr. 3rd		
	Homberg	-
Apr. 4th		
	Eschwege	-Apr.
7th		
	Treffurt	-
Apr. 10th		
	Gotha	-Apr.
11th Ordruff		

Concentration Camp Weimar		-
Apr. 13th. Buchenwald	Concentration Camp	
Bamberg		-
Apr. 20th		
Hersbuck		-
Apr. 22nd		
Burglengenfeld		-
Apr. 26th		
Regensburg		-
Apr. 28th		
Aufhausen (Bavaria)		-
May 2nd		
Ried (Austria)		-
May 5th		

In all they had liberated four concentration camps. In one camp, Ordruff, when they got there the Germans had shot all the people. The prisoners all had a cup in their hand and they were told to stand in line because they were going to feed them. When they all got in line the Germans machine gunned them all.

At this Camp they were greeted by a released inmate who volunteered to show them around the Camp. He would point out various areas of interest and say the Bosch did this or did that. They became very suspicious because the inmate seemed to be in very good health in comparison to the majority of the inmates in the camp.

Harry said that the next day when they showed up at the camp they found a man lying on the ground and his head was all swollen up and he said he thought he looked familiar. It was the man that had showed them around the day before. Several prisoners that had escaped from the camp came back and explained who he was. He had been severely beaten and then they found out that he was a very notorious German guard and the released prisoners had killed him. He had put on prisoners garb in an attempt to hide his identity.

He said that at these concentration camps there weren't very many German guards and that the prisoners had their own gardens. They made the prisoners do everything, including picking up the dead and burning them, etc.

The first American and also enemy casualties he seen was in France. An outfit was tied down and some members were sent to the rear to get ammunition. When they returned they were told not to cross this river to their outfit because they had all been captured. That wasn't the case so many were killed and wounded due to the lack of ammunition.
General Patton was really upset and wanted to know who had told them that they had been captured and said that if he found out he would shoot the SOB.

He said his outfit was the brains of the 20th Corp, 3rd Army even though nobody knew it because they weren't allowed to tell any one. Their job was solely to intercept German communications and pass it along to intelligence. His company commander was from Massillon and he would get so shook up when Patton came around he'd get drunk and one of his lieutenants would have to take over. Harry said he thought his commander died from alcohol but some years later he seen the Commander's mother in Massillon and she thought he had died from bad water. Patton was a scary guy, he said that he respected what he did, he probably did it the best way, but he sure didn't care about us. Sometimes his outfit would be the first one to get into a town. Some other outfit would be scheduled to get into the town but they would get held up along the way and they would end up in the town before them.

After the war he was shipped home landing at Camp Shanks, N.Y. where they were given a big steak dinner and issued some funds. He was sent to Indiantown Gap Military Reservation, Pennsylvania where he was discharged on the 29th of October 1945.

His rank when he was discharged was T-4 (Technical Sergeant)

His decorations and citations were – American Campaign Medal, European African Middle Eastern Service Medal with 4 Bronze Stars, World War II Victory Medal and Ruptured Duck Lapel Button.

A couple of his closest buddies were William Poore, Kentucky and Gale Hall (deceased)

He was employed at Faultless Rubber Co., Ashland, OH., where he made hot water bottles. Upon retirement he worked for F. E. Myers Co. and Ashland College in maintenance.

He married Betty Roesel November 12, 1946 and they were blessed with five children.

Gale Shire -   1947
Gloria Shire -   1949
Dwayne Shire - 1950
Roberta Shire - 1952
Harry Shire, Jr – 1954

Harry H. Shire's service didn't end with his discharge from the U.S. Army on October 29, 1945. Included with his Veteran's History is two presentations that he made as Commander of the Disabled American Veterans, Ashland, Ohio Chapter 81. I considered them excellent enough to include them.

MEMORIAL DAY
May 25, 1992

When ever I think of Memorial Day, I picture a bugler near a hillside grave, and I see a Veteran receiving his final call.

I hear the echo of the gun salute ringing through the air and the sobs of grief as the folded flag is handed to the Veteran's spouse.

I feel a jumping in my chest because my throat is blocked by a knot I can't explain. I fee a deep sense of gratitude to this Veteran, but how can I tell this person?

I can say a prayer and hope it is heard. No matter when or where or what war this Veteran served in, a dear price was paid for the sweet freedom we now enjoy. Freedom is not cheap. Ask the families of the Veterans we are about to remember this Memorial Day and don't forget tomorrow that we saluted them today.

We have an unbreakable bond formed with America, and no matter how often our country has called, people have stepped forward to defend it. We have never failed the call to arms.

Some people seem to forget very quickly the price these Veterans paid so we can walk free in this land, but the Veteran can't forget the loss of an arm or leg, or sometimes much more of their body.

The Veteran is led to believe that when they come home and they have problems, they will be taken care of or helped in some way. However, getting help from the government is almost another war in itself.

On any given night as many as 150,000 to 250,000 Veterans have no place to call home.

The equipment in our V.A. Hospitals is not the most modern and what there is is not in the best of shape. Broken equipment is not being replaced. A lot of the so-called doctors are interns or doctors that should be retired due to age. There aren't enough nurses to do the job properly.

Let's not forget the Prisoners of War and the Missing In Action. Where are the 78,000 missing from World War 11, the 8,800 from Korea, and the 2,300 from Vietnam? Could all of these Veteran's have just vanished?

The government said finding these military personnel was their highest priority. Where could they be looking? I could give them a clue, they are not it the White House.

We come together on this day to remember our Veterans, and remember we must.

We have many dates on paper that say w war has ended, but for a Veteran of a war, it will never end. You can't erase the memories of your mind. Only when our last breath has gone will it be over.

The Disabled Veterans will go on lying in their beds looking at the ceiling, or sitting in a wheel chair, or limping along through life remembering what it was like before they got in their condition. On Memorial Day, let's try to remember them. I'm sure they will remember you. Memories are about all some disabled Veterans have left.

Help celebrate Memorial Day. See the parade.

Harry H. Shire

Commander of Disabled Veterans

Ashland Chapter 81

MEMORIAL DAY 1993

A time to remember what freedom really means. Ask yourself, what does freedom mean to me? We in America have been free for so long, we have forgotten what tyranny and suppression can do to a nation.

We have not always been free. Many years ago the brave people of this great land we call America decided they would no longer be held in bondage. They came together under what we would call very crude conditions and fought for the rights and freedom we now enjoy.

Memorial Day is a day of rememberance, set aside to decorate the graves of Veterans that bought our freedom with their valor. Millions of Veterans have answered the call to arms and stood up for our freedom.

When the parade with our flag goes by, do you think it would be too great of an effort to stand and place your hand over your heart, and just for a moment think of those that gave their lives for our nations cause? It would make you feel better about yourself and teach our children there is still some respect left in this world. Almost everyone has lost someone in a war in the past.

The Memorial Day parade is representing all the Veterans of the past and those still living. Veterans don't like to be forgotten after they have done their best to save our country. It sometimes make them wonder, was it worth it all if no one cares?

It's imparitive to pass this respectfulness for our flag and country on to our children so they will remember why and how this freedom was won for them.

Most of the people of this world watch America and wonder at all the wonderful things we have in this country.

Why do we have so much discontentment and violence? Because all that most of them know about us is what the media tells them, which is mostly the bad things that happen in our country. It's about time to show some of our good side so all will understand we are a strong and united nation or one day, like the three bears, we may find someone eating our porridge, sitting in our chair, or sleeping in our bed and there is no way to know where we may be!

That's what is happening in many nations at this very time and they are crying "HELP". Help us anyone, Help, we are dying where we stand!

That's why we must show the world we are strong, so this will never happen to America. We shouldn't need so may planes, tanks, ships and rockets in our arsenal if we show the world we love our country and we mean to protect it no matter what.

Many people believe what they do in their life time will have no effect on what happens to our world, but we all do harm and we can also do good. Just remember "you" are the only "you" that has ever lived or ever will live. There will never be another you, so do the best you can while you have the chance. You may be surprised.

Help celebrate Memorial Day and see the parade.

Harry H. Shire
Commander of Disabled Veterans
Ashland Chapter 81

WILLIAM JOHN SKOMROCK, Sr.

William J. Skomrock, 15305 Munn Road, Novelty, Ohio 44072

He was born August 3, 1928 in Newbury, Ohio

He graduated from Newbury High School in 1946.

Bill became a part of the National Guard out of Chagrin Falls, Ohio #3641 Ordnance MAM (Medium Automotive Maintenance) Company. He joined shortly after High School. He attended several summer camps before he became activated into the regular Army in September 11, 1950. He had attained the rank of Sergeant before he became activated. Our unit trained with the regular Army at Camp Atterbury prior to any assignments during the Korean conflict which subjected all of our unit to call at will. During our Camp Atterbury, Indiana stay we were attached to the 5th Army and the Pennsylvania Keystone Division and participated in many ways as instructors in basic and automotive maintenance. He was also instructed by other people. They picked up a lot of draftees in their outfit, regular army draftees, from Michigan. They had a lot of College boys that came in and from West Virginia, Virginia and from the south and they had quite a few soldiers come in. They had basic training and then Automotive training, medium automotive training from heavy wreckers down to jeeps.

Bill with a couple of other Sergeants went down to Camp Connaly, Atlanta General Depot, Georgia and trained for medium automotive maintenance. They had large companies, six hundred men in a company training. The Master Sergeant who was in charge of them selected him for company drills on Saturdays. A West Point Colonel who was in charge of the base liked to have close order drills. Close order drill with six hundred men in a company was terrible because you had to have a twelve or sixteen man front and all the different commands. He said that he knew how to do it so he was selected to perform the task. Yelling the commands to such a large company he said that his neck size went up pretty heavy. He said that he liked it and also the automotive training.

Then back to Atterbury, which was their home base, for just a short time when they got ready for POM (Prior Overseas Maintenance) to Camp McCoy, Wisconsin. While there they were POMing equipment for Europe. There were self propelled guns, 155mm rifles, 105mm weapons which were all track vehicles like a tank. Very heavy with steel chevron tracks and they had to put on rubber padded tracks. They had to change a lot of engines and such. The big ones had a 540 Horse Power Radial Continental nine cylinder engine. Then they had to test them and load them onto rail cars and shipped them to Europe. They worked along side some civilians but they were isolated in that they were working only on the self propelled guns, and some trucks.

Upon completions there they came back to Atterbury again where they prepared for overseas shipment of their group to Thule, Greenland. Right on top of the world. They left Camp Atterbury by train to Norfolk, Virginia and boarded the U. S. General Stewart Heintzelman Ship and traveled with a convoy of thirty ships.

They could only go there in the summer by ship because it is all glaciers en-route. Greenland is a large continent with an average of only three miles of coast line, the rest is all glacier. Thule was the Northernmost occupied outpost with fifty Eskimos, two hundred fifty sled dogs and six Danish weathermen there in the post. They went into Thule Bay and built a five thousand foot runway. A short runway was built before they got there. The runway was excavated out of the edge of the Bay. There was twelve hundred feet of thermo frost in that area. They took out about four foot and put aggregate in and steam heated the whole five thousand feet with oil fired steam. It became like a floating pad on top of all this thermo frost. Bills position there was an automotive maintenance set up to maintain all the automotive equipment. They unloaded ships and did maintenance on vehicles. The way they did this is they took six or so hulls of LST ships that were never completed and they run them to ground and cabled them there. Then they put four cranes on each one of them to unload ships. A big convoy was run and never stopped. There were thirty ships all with steel and equipment. Then they brought in LSD's (Landing Ship Docks) with DUKW's, two an a half ton six by six DUKW's, just like a two and a half ton truck that floats. That was one of the big maintenance things that they had to do in Greenland, maintaining these DUKW's. They were used to handle small loads from ship to shore.

In Greenland in the summer time the temperatures ran from zero to forty degrees in the sun and in the summer the sun never set. It was hard to get your bearings because the sun just went around in circles. Strange things would happen like ice would move in from the sea and when the ice would move into the bay all the ships would have to move out. When on shore you were stuck without food or anything else. They lived on board ship. They lived on the Heintzelman when they got there and on the Casa Grande, a LSD, a navy ship which he liked, but it took to go ashore to work a twelve hour shift three hours to get to shore and three hours to get back. That didn't leave to much time for rest. He had a thirty man platoon that worked with him and every time they weren't doing something they would all go to sleep. He had to stay awake to make sure every body was safe.

They traveled back and forth on a LCVP (Landing Craft Vehicle Personnel) or a LCM (Landing Craft Machinery). The Navy did a good job. At times in the summer there was about twelve foot of tide. He remembered one time the navy tied up by the LST he was on and had to go to the CB Center for something and when they got back their boat was about fifty foot from the water. It was called operation BLUE JAY. They received a lot of good music from Russia and a lot of rhetoric about how all their girl friends back home were acting as reported by Moscow Molly. It was good to hear anything up there because reception wasn't good. Sending and receiving mail wasn't very good either. A letter home would take about two months to get there.

The aircraft would come in and bring all kinds of material and equipment but not some of the things such as mail that the troops would think of as essential. When a cargo plane would come in especially before they completed the long runways, they had to land by instruments and reverse feather the props and rev up the engines to keep from overshooting the runway. They did an excellent job. When Arctic Fog would move in you could stand about a foot away from each other and not make out the features and the water would just run off of you. Without explanation it would come and go.

As at any major construction accidents happens and they had a few but one Bill mentioned was that they had some equipment in their motor pool that they issued out to different Army outfits, CB's, etc. and they had two Model 29's Weasels. There was a group of fellows came in, an officer and four others, five guys altogether, and wanted a Weasel to go out along side the river alongside the glacier with it. They were told it wasn't a floatable machine but they tried to float it and it killed four out of the five. They were about six miles out along the river and they had to go up and recover the bodies. The river was run off from the Glaciers traveling to the sea. We remember recovering one of the men who was a Master Sergeant and he was a Master Sergeant at the time. He was only in about three feet of water but he was frozen into a fetal position. The others were in deeper water.

They had four cranes on each of the LST's and they had Euclid Trucks, seventeen yard trucks and they had about forty or fifty of them. They didn't do maintenance on them but they did have to help unload them. They had some floating cranes and everything had to float to get there but the Army, CB's and Navy did a great job of setting up everything. He said that people don't realize that it is like building Hoover Dam only in a smaller scale. It was just an unbelievable undertaking.

Bill said that he was just lucky because some of his outfit went to Korea. At least he was spared that experience.

Bill says he thinks that they are still maintaining that base. He felt that they had something underground there also, that nobody knew about. They weren't allowed to have cameras but some managed to have some. He does have pictures of some of the shipping. There was some strategic landscape that they didn't want pictures of such as a cone shaped mountain that looked like a volcano to the left side of the harbor. They were watched pretty close.

They were there in the summer of 1951. Going out of Norfolk Harbor it took them thirty one days to get to Thule. The North Atlantic was full of ice and the ships had to zig zag around the ice floes. They were in a straight line convoy and as they got further up north they would hit ice and the ships would circle and stay in touch. Two Ice Breakers were with them and it took a long time to get through. They ran into an ice berg when they were almost into Thule harbor. One of the boys from Chagrin Falls, Lester Green, came in and said that they were going to hit an ice berg. The ship started vibrating pretty bad because they put it in full speed reverse but sure enough they hit this ice berg. It didn't make a lot of noise but the bow of the ship went straight up in the air. There was sure a lot of whistles and bells. The Captain was anxious about stopping it. It went up then slid back down turning itself sideways and screwing itself into the ice. They had to shut everything down and the Captain anxiously checked for leaks. Fortunately there weren't any. They called in for the ice breakers because they had to go around to get it loose from the ice. Getting loose and starting up the propellers was sure noisy and raised concern about the condition of the drive shafts. It took about five or six hours to get them back and the convoy was pretty well separated so they were able to get back in. They were going in through a channel of ice that had been broken by the ice breakers and the ice looked like you would be able step off the ship and walk to shore. You couldn't tell what was shore and what was ice. The ice was all in pieces and just a mess. Bill was in compartment F-3 which was one deck above the bilges. F-3 was below the water line and the water was so cold that on the inside of their compartment was all ice. The salty ocean water on the outside was below thirty two degrees so the humidity on the inside created frost that covered the inside of the compartment. It was a scary thing especially being in that bow when the ship was pushing through all that ice. All the stays, the bow trusses, on the inside of the ship were so far apart and the skin between were all bent in from the ice. It was scary. The Navy did a great job. On the way up on the Heinselman some of the ships crew were civilians. One of the Chief Machinist Mates befriended our group. Up in the North Atlantic it got really rough and the bow of the ship would go right under water. There would be some ice bergs out and you couldn't tell how far away they were. You couldn't tell because there wasn't anything to reference to. So he had an old 1903 Springfield with tracers and he said he would shoot and you were to count one thousand one, etc. until the tracer reached the ice berg. The tracer averaged about two thousand foot per second so you could figure the distance. It was amazing because some of the ice bergs would look like they were about fifty feet from you and they would be a half a mile away. When they got farther up into the Atlantic the Captain turned off all Radar because it was worthless. It was all ice and all the Radar screen would show was snow. So then he would double the watch on the front and it was a good thing he did because when they hit that ice berg those guys were screaming their heads off.

When they left to come back from Greenland they just left everything there. They just signed it all over to NAC (North Atlantic Construction). They came home on the LSD (Landing Ship Dock) they came back on a flank run, full speed. They had gunnery practice on the way back, a five inch gun above their compartment. They would shoot some flack up and use all their pom-pom's and their forty millimeters and twenties shooting tracers at that flack. It was interesting and noisy. They came back to Norfolk, Virginia and got on a train back to Camp Atterbury. Bill said that when they were shipping out they traveled to Norfolk on a coal fired train hauling all their equipment along. Going home they traveled on a diesel train without any equipment. When they got back to Camp Atterbury they stayed through the winter and took a lot of training. They wanted to keep us busy. He was in a barracks with seven Master Sergeants and he was the lowest ranking Master Sergeant so they put him in charge because they didn't want to do anything. He said that they were doing all kinds of odd ball jobs awaiting to be discharged. One thing he did was to move a machine shop from Sault saint Marie, Michigan back to Camp Atterbury. It was one of several per diem type jobs that he did. He went across the Mackinac Strait with an ice breaker with the machine shop.

He received his discharge at Camp Atterbury on May 7, 1952 and he was anxious to get out because he wanted to get married and his girlfriend did to.

He was married June 14, 1952 to Mary Louise Fife.

They have three children, two boys and a girl, William, Lynn and Jefrey.

CLAIR DWIGHT STOTLAR

Clair Dwight Stotlar,12287 Lela Lane, Burton, Ohio 44021

Born November 19, 1930, Whipple, Ohio in Washington County

Graduated from Bainbridge High School (Geauga County) in 1948

He enlisted in the United States Air Force, September 1950. Basic training was done at Lackland Air Force Base and Shephard Air Force Base in Texas.

After basic, he was flown to Lowry Air Force Base in a C-46 aircraft, for technical training. Training was in aerial photography and camera maintenance. Training was from October, 1950 to February, 1951.

His first assignment was at O'Hare Air Force Base in Chicago, Illinois at the base Photo Lab. He was there for nineteen months, from February 1951 through September 1952.

He was sent to Korea to serve with the 429th Fighter Bomber Squadron of the 49th Fighter Bomber Wing stationed at K-2 Air Base at Taegu. He was the senior camera technician for the Squadron. He was responsible for all of the 16mm gun cameras. Each F-84 airplane was equipped with a camera for recording bomb and strafing missions. At night North Korean troops would enter the base to scrounge for food. The Base Commander feared for the safety of the airmen and issued M-2 Carbines. That didn't last long as some of the airmen got drunk and started shooting up the airmen's club. The carbines were recalled immediately. After the Armistice was signed, he was invited by the Navy to be their guest aboard the aircraft carrier "Boxer" for an R&R trip to Hong Kong. The Navy pilots put on a show off the coast of Formosa to impress the Chinese. He watched the show from the bridge. He was a member of an Air Force gunnery team that traveled all over Korea on a C-47 aircraft. The Air Force pilots competed with the Marines and Navy pilots in aerial gunnery. Fifty caliber ammunition was color coded for each of the services, so that each team could be scored.

One of his tough jobs was to make frequent trips to Japan for camera parts and supplies.

His last assignment was with March Air Force Base, Riverside, California from 1953 to his discharge in September 28th,1954. Upon his arrival at the March Air Force Base he was asked if he would like to join his new outfit that had been sent to Upper Heyford Air Base in England. He agreed and spent four months there on TDY. It was a B-47 bomber base. The weather and smog were so bad, that the aircraft were flown to Africa and the missions were conducted from there. The missions consisted of photo reconnaissance and precision bomb drops. All landings at Upper Heyford were (ILS) Instrument Landings. After returning to March Air Force Base, he was chosen as a member of a B-47 jet survey team traveling to the Far East. He flew on a KC-97 refueling aircraft to Hawaii, Guam, Midway, Kwajalein, Okinawa and Tokyo. The team stayed at each location long enough to insure that facilities were in place to handle large jet bombers. The tankers were not equipped to handle passengers, so parachutes were used for seats. On take-off from March, the airplane traveled through a flock of birds. Whenever the heat was turned on, the smell of burning birds make it intolerable. It was a very long and cold trip to Hawaii.

Returning to his home base at March Air Force Base he completed his tour of duty by participating in aerial photography.

Upon returning home he took advantage of the Bill of Rights by attending Kent State University, majoring in Geology and Biology and graduated in 1961.

He married Jean Niemi from Ashtabula, Ohio on August 31, 1957.

He now has two sons, two daughters- in- law and five,(soon to be six), grandchildren.

He worked as a research metallurgist, while earning a teaching certificate at Cleveland State University. He taught science and aviation at Newbury High School. A number of his aviation students became pilots. He has a vintage airplane, which he restored.

His service ribbons consists of the Good Conduct Medal, National Defense Service Medal, Korean Service Medal with 2 Bronze Stars, United Nations Service Medal and the Korean Medal issued by South Korea fairly recently.

He was discharged with the Rank of Staff Sergeant.

His service comrade is Gary Martell from Bainbridge. They are still very good friends.

ROBERT J. SULYOK

Robert J. Sulyok, 109 Lakeview Lane, Chagrin Falls, Ohio 44022

He was born September 11, 1932 in Cleveland, Ohio

Bob didn't graduate before he went into the service but he did get his GED and after his service time he went back to Mayfield High and they issued him a Diploma in 1954.

He Enlisted in the United States Marine Corp on the 23rd of February, 1951.

He entered boot camp at Paris Island which lasted twelve weeks. After some tests it was determined that he tested quite high and they had him fill out a form asking what he would like to do. His brother had told him that they very seldom ever gave you your first choice. He wanted to be in radio so he made it his second choice. He made the infantry his first choice and radio his second. Sure enough they signed him up for Radio School. They sent him to Radio School in San Diego starting near the end of June. He learned Morse Code and learned to type. He said that he had never learned to type but became very proficient in typing and was able to type fifty words per minute. He said that by the time he finished school around the first of December he was receiving fifty words a minute in Morse Code, sending thirty five words per minute and typing fifty words per minute without error.

While in San Diego he said that he made a lot of friends in both the Air Force and the Navy by going into the YMCA. The YMCA always had something going for the men.

From San Diego he came home for Christmas and then went back to Camp Pendleton and then shipped out to Korea. First they went to Kobe, Japan and had one day of liberty there then went back on board to Inchon, Korea. They were sent from Inchon up front to division headquarters. He was in the first Signal Battalion, Headquarters Battalion, First Marine Division. He was always attached to them except for temporary assigned duty to go back to Aschom City where they made landings on islands. They called them shore parties, shore parties use to be called CB's in the second world war. They were working together with British forces,

Australian forces and a couple members of Sweden. A United Nations force. They were Island hopping and if there were enemy on the island they would capture them or annihilate them. Their job was to set up ship to shore communications and air communications. That is where he received one commendation because things happened and they came through without any problems at all. They also worked with Sikorsky Helicopters and he made several trips with them over enemy terrain. They used them for gun ships also. They mounted them with thirty caliber and fifty caliber machine guns. He said that they were one of the first ones to use them as attack ships rather that just recovery of wounded. One flight failed and they came down on just rotary and they bounced pretty hard. The engine just stalled out. Nobody was hurt. It did break the landing gear and the prop chewed up all the terrain around them.

They were in Jong Churi, to the Thirty Eighth Parallel, In Pan Mon Jong setting up communications. It was one of the last jobs he had setting up communications so that they could exchange prisoners. They called it Freedom Village. He left before the prisoner exchange.

They were supposed to come home in April when Pork Chop Hill got hit real bad so that every one scheduled to go home got back on the trucks and headed back to the front. Some of the guys didn't make it. The following month they came home. They went from Korea to Sasebo, Japan. Sasebo during WW11 was a big naval yard where the enemy built their ships. This is where stories were told how American submarines would stand off shore waiting for new ships to be built and sunk them as they came out of the harbor. Then they shipped out and landed at Treasure Island, California. It took four or five days for papers to be processed for them to go home on leave. While waiting they were able to go on leave to San Francisco where they would go to the Marines Club on State Street. Before going to the Marines Club they found a restaurant where they would all go and order Steak and Milk. They had them put the quart bottles of milk on the table. He said that they probable drank more milk than they ate steak. Then on to the Marines Club. While waiting to go home they took care of everybody on the base, to fly out or take the train. Six of them decided that they would arrange their own transportation home because if they depended on the base they would probable send them home on a slow troop train. So they all went into town and went to the train station and bought their tickets there. They got on the Santa Fe Line and it took two days to go from San Francisco to Chicago and another eight hours from Chicago to Cleveland. It was a good choice because they were the only service men on the train and all the nice civilians were treating them to every thing.

They had a thirty day leave and then went to Lejeune and while at Camp Lejeune he was teaching radio. Then while teaching radio they had exercises down on Puerto Rico for landing operations training. They called it

Advance Combat Training. Bob and four officers flew down out of Cherry Point, N.C. They got half way out into the Caribbean when one of the engines starts burning. They were flying out in a flying boxcar with two engines that had just been released with other problems. They were told to put on their parachutes and one of the officers was really scared. Bob said that he was calculating how much money he would get for the jump, money for rescue and another thirty day leave. He was only nineteen or twenty at that time so he was thinking that was the best deal he ever had. Fortunately they made it to an Air Force Base with the engine still burning and they were all ready for them with foam and fire trucks spraying foam on them as they were landing. By the time they came to a stop the engine was out. He was on Puerto Rico seven days and then came home on ship.

Then he received his discharge the twenty second of February, 1954 from H&S Company, 8th Marines, 2nd Marine Division, fleet Marine Force, Camp Lejeune, North Carolina. When he originally arrived at Camp Lejeune he drove is own car from Cleveland and that's how he got home.

The Marine Corp wanted him to stay in and he said that he wanted to stay in and be a life time Marine but his wife to be didn't want that kind of life.
Then after he was home about three months the C.I.A. sent him a letter wanting him to work for them, because

of his Marine Corp experience and the efficiency marks that came with it, his conduct and also what he did. They wanted him to set up communications in South America. His wife didn't want that either. He said that he became a full fledged civilian but in his heart he has always stayed a Marine. He said that the older he gets the prouder he is for having served with the men he served with and what they have done because that is what he has done. That makes him proud that he is one of them.

Bob married Shirley Greggs July 17, 1954. 2004 is their fiftieth year.

They had two girls who are now 46 and 39 and four grand children, 22, 19, 11 and 7.

His medals consisted of Korean Service Medal with two stars, National Defense Service Medal, United Nations Service Medal & Ribbon and Good Conduct Medal. He received a commendation from the Korean President, the Korean Presidential Unit Citation, United States Marine Corp Service Commemorative Medal and Cold War Victory Medal. Then the Over Seas Service Commemorative Medal with ribbon struck to honor all soldiers, sailors, Marines and airmen in overseas theatre or expeditionary operations outside the United States for thirty days or more.

Bob went to Fenn College under the G.I. Bill

He retired from Sears, Roebuck and Company after twenty seven years in September 1997.

He belongs to Veterans of Foreign wars, American Legion, Marine Corp League and a member of the Marine Honor Guard. He is also active with the Frozen Chosin.

He still keeps in touch with some of his buddies from Inchon.

STANLEY PETER TALARCEK

Stanley P. Talarcek, 8883 Fairmount Road, Novelty, Ohio 44072

He was born May 2, 1925 in Claridon, Ohio

He attended several schools and left the Russell, Ohio school in the eleventh grade to join the Navy. He only needed one credit in Civics to graduate and when he returned from the services he was encouraged to take the test, which he passed easily, acquiring the one credit and receiving his diploma.

Stanley's brother went into the army and was sending him letters and pictures of where he was stationed in the desert in California and on the basis of his brothers experiences he decided that the Army was not his choice of service. He enlisted in the U. S. Navy at the age of seventeen. Another occasion that motivated him to join the Navy was seeing a friend of the family who was in the Navy in his white uniform. Seeing his friend in that white uniform made an impression on him to join the Navy.

He enlisted in the Navy April 30, 1943 and entered active service on May 3, 1943. He went to the Great Lakes Naval Station for his boot camp and while there the guy that did the interviewing informed him that the best job in the Navy was as an electrician. So the interviewer wrote down on his records that his hobby was in electrics and in school he had industrial arts in electricity.

After Boot Camp he was sent down to Morehead State Teachers College, Morehead, Kentucky where they had an electrical school. He took a course in basic electrics for sixteen weeks. He was then sent to Brooklyn, New York to a Gyro_Compass School for thirteen weeks. At the Gyro school there was a Chief Electrician who took a liking to him and told him to put in for a troop transport. He said that you eat like a king and you are protected by the whole fleet in transporting troops. When the charts came up those with the highest grades got first choice of which ship they would like to board. There were about thirty ships and thirty students looking for emplacement. Stanley noticed that one transport was called the

Starlight and he thought it had a nice romantic name so he chose it.

He joined the crew of the U.S.S. Starlight AP 175 at Staten Island, N. Y. It was built in South Carolina and sent to Staten Island for refurbishing to a Hospital ship and troop transport. They embarked to go through the Panama Canal and when they got close they saw a line of ships about ten miles long waiting to go through the canal. He thought they would be in line for ever but to his surprise his ship passed all of them and went right through the canal. They went through to the other side and they had a one day lay over in Panama City. They had shore leave and three of the crew got pulled off the ship for having a fight ashore. While ashore they went to a shop who sold pillow cases, scarves and other items and being young and innocent they purchased some items for the store to ship home for them. The shop keeper promised to get them shipped immediately and placed them under the counter without asking for the addresses, which should have told them something but they paid and left. Nothing ever arrived at their homes.

From Panama they went to Hawaii along with two destroyers, refueling the destroyers twice along the way. When they arrived at Hawaii, before they could go into the harbor, they had to throw over the side all the storage batteries, all five inch ammunition and all the five gallon paint cans. Not until some time later on the History Channel did he find out the reason. Just prior to their arriving there they had a bunch of LST's that were getting ready for the invasion of Saipan and about ten of them burnt. A welding job on one ship set the ship on fire and they being all tied up together they all burned. They had to get torpedo boats in to sink them to prevent more damage to nearby LST's. In fear of a reoccurrence they had to make incoming vessels dump certain items. It was kept a secret until the 80's.

From there they went to Guam unloading troops and bringing casualties out and back to Pearl Harbor where they had to dump everything all over again. Later after this they never had this problem in reentering the harbor. Upon leaving Hawaii about the second day out the forced draft blowers shut down. They had to drop back from the fleet until they corrected the problem. They were only going about eight or nine knots instead of fifteen. They dropped back two destroyers with them. One forced draft blower wasn't working, it would start up then shut off. They had about twenty horse motors. They found out after working on it for about four hours that it wasn't the motor but the control. They changed relays but that didn't help so they took the panel off the wall and here they found that one of the wires was broken. They got it fixed about midnight and the skipper called them up on the bridge and had them bring out cots right on the bridge and told them to sleep right through general quarters, that no one would bother them. He brought out a quart of rum and told them to finish it and throw the bottle over the side because alcohol wasn't allowed on the Navy ships. About dawn he felt a guy straddling him looking at a repeater that took readings on each side of the ship so you didn't bump into another ship. The Quartermaster was taking a reading because they had already caught up to the fleet. He pushed his cot to the side, climbed into the Gyro Shack and went back to sleep. From Hawaii they went to Eniwetok, a staging area, where they took the 77th Army into Guam. They had the Army unloaded and on the beach by 8 A.M. and by noon they received Marine casualties. A LCT brought the Marine wounded alongside, on stretchers, on a pallet some twenty or thirty. They were winched aboard where deck hands lined the stretchers on the Starboard deck until they could be transferred to sick bay. On the second day he was surprised to see this big bright white ship, the hospital ship USS Hope, standing off shore. He was amazed to see it so bright and vulnerable. Volunteers were requested for the casualties and Stanley volunteered to help clean up the casualties. He said that he went down to sick bay and got a bucket of water and a towel and went up on deck to clean up the Marines. All the Marines on the stretchers weren't moving, they probably all had morphine shots. He started to wash this Marines face that was covered over with red lava mud. He said that he saw this young face, not moving, but like dead, and he started to cry. A hospital corpsman told him, "get the hell out of here, this isn't a job for you." He went back to the bridge. The dead were kept in the freezer and taken off at eniwetok with the rest taken to Pearl Harbor.

They came back to Pearl and got all set for the invasion of Yap. When two
days out to sea they were diverted to Leyte. They had found out that there were practically no Japs on the island of Leyte so they took the 34th Division into Leyte. Everything went like clock work, action in the distance but nothing close. Then from there they went to Biak, New Guinea to pick up replacements to bring back to Leyte because the Japanese were rushing reinforcements. While unloading reinforcements they had a message come over the P.A. system saying 'hold your fire, friendlies in the area'. Under this directive two Jap planes came in and they were looking at them coming in at about fifty feet above the water. One of the boys, an electrician, use to be a gunner in the Merchant Marines, said that he was going to practice leading these guys when all of a sudden they realized that they were Japanese and the young man on the gun mount with two burst dropped both planes. Just plain luck and the Starlight received a radio message from the Admiral saying 'Good shooting Starlight.' Soon after the American planes showed up and the whole fleet started shooting at them. Luckily they avoided them. From then on only real recognizable planes would fly over the fleet such as P 38's. The boys in the fleet were to trigger happy.

Then they picked up troops on New Guinea and they practiced landings on Empress Bay. Then they went to

Manus a British Island right off New Guinea. While there they were surprised to have to pay a nickel for coffee or orange juice to the Red Cross. Usually every where they went they received coffee or whatever, free. They were at Manus over Christmas and while the skipper left the ship the medics brought out the alcohol and they mixed it with grapefruit juice. They had troops on the ship and almost every one got drunk. Stanley doesn't drink but no one got into any fights, they were all as happy as a lark.

Being that he was a Gyro technician, every month he was given a pint of grain alcohol for cleaning purposes because it didn't leave any residue. He had a tool box with a lock on it that he kept it in and there were a couple of drunks on the ship and every time he went for the alcohol he would find it replaced by carbon tetrachloride.

The Gyro shack was located right behind the wheel house so that was where he spent most of his time above the water line in case of a torpedo attack. He even took a mattress on the deck of the Gyro shack and he slept there. The Gyro_Compass was the brains of the ship which assured the ship was on course and was maintaining proper distance from other ships. In the Gyro shack Stanley had pictures on the wall from home and also of Jane Russell from the movie the Outlaw. The Skipper was US Navy Reserve and not as regulated and he would come into the Gyro shack and look around at all his pictures without paying a lot of attention to an inspection.

At Mindoro Island in the Philippines they unloaded every one in eight hours and got out of there as fast as they could because there were to many suicide bombers in the area. From there they went to Espirito Santo in the New Hebrides. On the way down one of the relays on the compass went down. He spent most of his time on the bridge hanging out with the guys up there. He would be exchanging pleasantries with the Radio man in the radio shack and all the time they would be talking he would be typing up code he was receiving. While talking with the Junior Officers they looked back behind the ship and noticed that the wake was in kind of a circle. Then they noticed that the compass was about five degrees left rudder. The Steerman said that he had a five degree right rudder and it was still going left. The ship was slowly making a curve. They changed to manual compass and disconnected the relay. They went into Espirito Santo on the magnet compass and hit it right on. They couldn't get a new relay there but taking it to an electric shop they were able to fix it immediately.

From Biak they made the invasion of Luzon. At Luzon in the Lingayen Gulf when they got in there had been a storm and the water was smooth but there were these huge rollers and the troops had a problem getting off the ship. Luckily no one was hurt. After the invasion Japanese suicide boats were running down this river attempting to ram our ships. They were destroyed leaving large boxes floating in the water and it was said that Japanese were hiding under the boxes. There was so much debris floating in the water that it looked like you could walk ashore on it. Riflemen were shooting all night from the ships through the boxes and bullets were ricocheting from the water driving everybody below decks. Some guys got hurt so shooting was ordered stopped. They sat in the Lingayen Gulf for four or five days and they got credit for two more Japanese planes. The Boise was anchored right behind them and where he was located he could see that a Kamikaze was heading straight for them about twenty feet above the water. The Boise was handicapped in that they couldn't just fire within the fleet for fear of hitting other vessels. The Japanese always tried to hit destroyers or bigger ships instead of cargo or troop ships. He could see the Boise's five inch weapons moving toward the plane and when it got within a couple of hundred feet all the guns went off and the plane just stopped and disintegrated right before your eyes. They must have been using proximity fuses. They all met the plane and exploded at the same time with instant destruction.

When they were at Okinawa and just sitting there waiting in reserve the suicide planes were just constantly coming over. They were there about four or five days when they sent them about forty or fifty miles up the island to unload at a different place. They were traveling with two destroyers when two Japanese planes came in and the destroyers were shooting at them. The Starlight got credit for two more Japanese planes. The destroyers were zig zaging and one of the planes burst into a ball of flame and was heading straight for one of the destroyers. The crew started jumping overboard because they thought for sure it was going to hit. Instead it overshot the destroyer. After that the destroyer turned around and picked up the crew. The second destroyer was missed by the second plane by a long shot. The pilot must have been already dead.

Stanley said that they credited the Starlight for 8 ½ planes shot down but officially in the record they only have 6.

At Okinawa, they were there for almost a week, every day they would announce bogies coming in. There would be almost a hundred at a time but very seldom did any make it through. They would get shot down by the Navy carriers. Maybe a dozen out of a hundred would ever get over the fleet.

They had a problem with bugs on the ship especially weevils in the bread. They would hold the bread up to the light and pick the bugs out. They got some Marines aboard and they told them about the bugs but they didn't care they ate them anyway. Stanley said that the Marines must have been trained on bugs. After about a month of this they put raisins in the bread, so they had raisin bread till they got back to the states.

After Okinawa they went straight to the states, crossing the International Date Line on May 2nd Stanley's birthday. Two birth dates in two days. As soon as they got in the states the ship was decontaminated.

Being in the service and connected with the electrical group they use to go and check out the skippers freezers to make sure the fans were working in his freezer. Two of them would always go and they would shove about a dozen eggs inside their shirt. They would have eggs all the time.

When going down to the New Hebrides they crossed the equator and the Skipper and about twenty 'OLD SALTS' had crossed the equator prior on other ships but the rest of his crew had never crossed over. So the Skipper made a big deal out of it, a real initiation. They performed all kinds of crazy stunts. The worst thing was a Commander who was an older person was given a five gallon pail of lard and he had to crawl through a wind tunnel, which was about thirty foot long, pushing this can of lard ahead of him painting the insides with lard. He made it through but he was so dripping wet from the heat and sweating that he looked as though he just came out of the water. The meals had to be made by the Officers. The whole day was just a lot of fun.

Upon leaving the Philippines they picked up a part of the Sixth Marines in the New Hebrides and then went over to Guadalcanal and picked up some more Marines. Then they went via Manus and Peleliu to Ulithi and on to Okinawa.

After the war they took CB's into Sasebo, Japan and the inlet was about ten miles long and was lined with ships waiting to get in and unload. Here they were passing them all up right up to the dock. Passing a long line of catcalls from crews waiting in line. The CB's were being brought there to build docks.

After being decontaminated in the states they took troops out to the Philippines and on the way out to the Philippines they had some excitement with a submarine. The Destroyers were running around like crazy and finally destroyed the submarine.

A couple of times they got into some severe weather and he got rolled out the bunk. He was told they got a 35 degree roll. 35 degrees with a transport is really something. In bad weather you could see Destroyers lying on their sides fairly often. They were built to withstand it. Coming back to the states they got into a severe storm and the Junior Officer on the deck never slowed down the ship and they run into a monstrous wave and it was like the ship ran into a brick wall. Stanley was sleeping in the Gyro shack and the Skipper came out of his cabin and started to chew out the officer for going to fast in bad weather.

After the war they made a trip to China, a couple of trips back and forth to Guam taking people over and bringing replacements back. They took replacements into China and anchored out into a bay and an LCT took them out to Tientsin about fifty miles up the river. They had a forty hour pass into Tientsin. In Tientsin they stayed in a hotel in the first and second floors. The six upper floors were all filled with residents of ill repute.

Stanley said that they ruined it for the Marines at Tientsin because when they came in they had to exchange American dollars for Chinese dollars. They got twenty four thousand Chinese dollars for every American dollar and when they left the exchange rate, in forty eight hours, went from one American dollar to thirty six thousand Chinese dollars. In other words instead of them having to exchange twenty four thousand Chinese dollars for one American dollar they had to exchange thirty six thousand Chinese dollars for one American dollar. Caused by the way the Americans spent money within the two days, it caused the difference in the exchange rate.

When they came back from China they brought back some high point Marines back to San Diego. Stanley was frozen at sixty four points while others were getting out with only forty points. They tried to talk him into re-enlisting offering him electrician first class if he would sign over. He said that he wanted out but now he says that if he would have been smart he would have stayed in. The Navigator, a full Lieutenant told him that if he could get some one to replace him with the Gyro he would let him off. There was a Striker, a feisty young kid that went on shore leave and was coming back just as the Skipper was leaving the ship. The Skipper Said 'Son you shouldn't do that' because he was coming back drunk. The Striker hollered to the Skipper 'Don't call me son, your not a relative of mine'. The Skipper didn't say anything. Stanley said that in five minutes he taught him everything he had learned in one year. He taught him basic functions. This would get him off but he wondered what happened when this young man would be spending most of his time on the bridge with the Skipper.

He managed to get off before the ship took off for Hong Kong. He got on a train and it took five days to get to the Great Lakes Naval Training Station. They traveled eating sandwiches and oranges arriving at night and they fed them, the first meal they had in five days. The next morning, as he said 'zip –zip- zip', you went through the inspections and received your discharge put on a train and you go home.

He was discharges March 20, 1946. His rate at time of discharge was EM 2c, Electricians Mate Second Class.

Stanley said that during his time in the service he got to enjoy some entertainment such as the Stage Door Canteen in Los Angeles and once he took a young lady to the Latin Quarter in New York. The Latin Quarter was owned by Barbara Walters father. They weren't afforded very good seats and the entertainer was the bandleader Ted Lewis of 'me and my shadow' fame. The meal came to $18.72 and he gave the waiter a twenty dollar bill and the waiter seemed to be rather irate. He turned and went back into the kitchen. When they went to leave he excused himself and went into the kitchen and asked the waiter for his change which didn't go over to good. The girl asked him if something was the matter and he informed her that the waiter forgot to give him his change. He was told that it was customary to tip the servers.

Another time they went to the Riverside Hotel in New York and they were greeted at the door. The place was packed but they were escorted up on stage and a table was set up for them about five yards up on the stage. Their food and drinks were provided free and the entertainment was provided by Dan Dailey, Mary Martin and Betty Boop.

He was guided to the Six Foot Club where every one there was six foot tall or over. Stanley said that he found it very difficult to dance with tall girls because they kept bumping knees.

This little old country boy in the services education was greatly enhanced.

The awards he earned were, Victory Medal, Philippine Liberation Ribbon (2 stars), Letter of commendation Bar (1 star), Asiatic Pacific Area Campaign Medal (4' stars)

He went to a radio school in Cleveland, Ohio under the G.I. Bill. Then he took up training in something new at the time – Television.

He married Jean Kubiak on May 1, 1948, the day before his birthday.

They were blessed with four children.

EARL WILLIAM WARNE

Earl W. Warne, 15080 Woodsong Drive, Middlefield, Ohio 44062

Born March 30, 1925 at Pittsburgh, Pennsylvania.

Earl lost his father when he was eleven years old and his mother was burdened in raising him and as he says, 'he was a brat, always getting into something, just full of it'. He had left home for a while but when the war broke out he came back home and told his mother that he was going to go into the service. He was only seventeen at the time. He and some of his friends from Parkman went into Cleveland and checked the Navy first and they wouldn't take them in. Then they went down to the Marine Corp, which was what he wanted to begin with, and they said OK but they would have to have his mothers signature of approval. She didn't want to sign but he kept pestering her until she finally gave in. Four of them went back in and joined, Rich Beard, Bruce Olmsted and Leland Gotham.

They entered the Marine Corp on February 2nd, 1943. He took his boot training at Paris Island and after he came out of there he said that he was a different person. He was still seventeen but he had a different attitude, outlook on life, the way he took care of himself and how he treated other people. In the Marine Corp training that is built into you. Even to this day he says he still carries on some of the training instilled into him in the Marine Corp. He says the service was very gratifying and he don't regret one bit of it.

In the Corp discipline and care of your equipment was of the greatest importance. Earl said that one time they were called out for short order drill for fifteen or twenty minutes. The sand would stir everything up and if you had just a little bit of oil or something in the barrel of our weapon it would cause the sand to cling to it. One day he had been in a hurry that night and he thought he had his rifle cleaned perfect. The Sergeant looked down in the barrel and he said 'what's in here Marine?' He said 'it's clean sir.' The Sergeant said 'what did you say! Look at this!' He looked and sand was clinging to some oil he had missed. The Sergeant commanded him to stack his rifle and bring over a bucket that was there. The Sergeant said 'now I want you to put this on your head and start running around this drill field and I want you to call out I'M A SHIT HEAD.' He started running and the Sergeant would holler 'I can't hear you.' Earl said that in that bucket it was vibrating and the Sergeant kept saying that he couldn't hear him and he ran around there for about fifteen minutes. He said it was about a hundred degrees out there and when he got through the sweat was pouring off his head. He said that every rifle was clean after that. That was the training that they had and it was important when you were landing on some beach in the sand, your life could depend on it. Earl claims that it was training such as this that he is here today.

On November 8th, 1943 he went to the Marine Corp Training Center, Camp Lejeune . New River, Hadnot Point, where he satisfactorily completed the prescribed Comsat intelligence course on December 4th. He was considered proficient in the following subjects:

Combat Intelligence
Scouting and Patrolling
Ground Observation
Elementary Map Reading
Military Sketching
Elementary Aerial Photograph Reading
Japanese Infantry Organization
Marine Corps Organization
Japanese Infantry Weapons
Rubber Boat Reconnaissance
Unarmed Combat
Intelligence Command Post Duties

Hydrographic Charts
Booby Traps
Counter Intelligence

He shipped out January 12th, 1944 to New Caledonia. He was only there less than a week when they moved to Puvuvu where he joined his outfit.

Puvuvu where he joined the First Marine Division on this Island that was supposed to be for R & R. The Division had just come out of Cape Gloucester, New Britain from combat and it was anything but a spot for rest and relaxation. It was nothing but rotting coconuts, land crabs, rats, toads and mud over your shoe tops. It was being set up as a rest area between combat tours. They did get there in time for the Bob Hope Show. Bob Hope and his group were flown in from the island of Benika in Piper Cubs. There was Bob, Jerry Colonna, Heda Hopper, Brown and his band of renown, a beautiful young lady dancer, Joan Evans and Frances Langford.

From Puvuvu they shipped out to Guadalcanal to regroup for movement to Peleliu. On Peleliu Earl landed in the third wave. He landed amongst mass confusion and destruction. Ernie Pyle was among his outfit and later on when he got back to Hawaii he went to see the cemetery where Ernie was buried. He served in action against the enemy on Peleliu from September 15th, 1944 to October 14th, 1944. From Peleliu they went back to Puvuvu arriving November 26. After some regrouping and training they left on February 28, 1945 for three days on Guadalcanal in preparation for Okinawa..

Earl said that he kind of regrets that he came out. He made a field promotion to Corporal on Peleliu. In the unit he was in there was about thirty men, unit R26, Scouts and Observers. It consisted of thirty members, two Sergeants, three Corporals and the rest were Privates and PFC's. Then you had One First Lieutenant, two Second Lieutenants and a Captain.

Earl said that they went out on a patrol one night and there were five of them. When they came back through the line of course they had to give the days password. When they got back and they have no idea when and how it happened, but they had one extra man. A Jap had got in with them and so Swede whispered to the guard that they had one extra man back there and he don't belong to us. He said 'do you want to take care of it?' They assured him that they would take care of it when he came through. So when he got to the line they asked him for the password and he couldn't speak English so they took care of him. They had a lot of nerve and it wasn't unusual for them to attempt things like this.

Earl's Commander when they hit the shore said that he wanted as many prisoners as possible. They went out on a patrol and there were quite a few of them and they got ambushed. They got out of there but one of the guys got shot and when they got out they started counting and found themselves one short. So they regrouped taking them about fifteen minutes and they went back in to see if they could find the one missing. The Japanies had captured him and they had cut his penis off and stuffed it in his mouth and they knew he was alive when they had done this. They had tied him up between two trees with wire around his fingers. They brought him back out with them and the word got out and there weren't any more prisoners taken.

On Peleliu their Company Headquarters was moving to a new location. Combat was moving forward so they had to move ahead, so they were going around toward the island of Ngesebus and had to go through this ravine to get to their new location. A Colonel was in charge of taking them down and this sniper, a machine gunner opened up and half of the patrol got through.

Earl said that after Peleliu they moved back to Puvuvu for R&R and It was as bad as the first time. They had to clean up the area and set up their camps. Coconuts, land crabs, rats and all were just as bad as the first time. And then they had a Typhoon and the water came through and they had quite a mess. At least on Puvuvu they kept them busy studying maps, etc. which kept them from standing guard duty and KP. Swede his sergeant would say they were going over to another island and do some maneuvering. He would send Earl to go down to Headquarters and pick up some supplies for them. He would say to line up a LCVP (landing craft vehicle personnel) for them with supplies. He said that they would go over to this other island, get set up and the work they did was boar hunt. They had their rubber boats and they would go out in the bay between the islands. The water was perfectly clear and beautiful, you could see clear to the bottom. They would throw grenades over the side and when fish would come up they would grab them. They caught a wild boar and they had him on a roaster and cooked him all night long.

Once they got on an island where they confined lepers. He thought what have they got themselves into. It's the worst and saddest sight you ever wanted to see. They didn't stay long because they had just went there to observe what was on the island.

Earl said that after Puvuvu and Guadalcanal they arrived at Ulithi Beach, Okinawa were he served in action from April 1, 1945 to June 21st, 1945. When in Okinawa and his unit seized Shuri Castle and the fortress city, Earl and his buddy PFC Joe T. Morris came across a deserted Japanese truck. There was a little damage to it but the two of them with a little mechanical ingenuity was able to fix it up and with the permit of their Commanding Officer they drove all over Okinawa hauling food and water for the troops. Once when Earl was hunting for firewood he came across a Jap standing in the brush. He jumped out of his truck and managed to wound the Jap who took off with Earl following until he caught up with him and was able to finish him off before the Jap managed to use a grenade. He and some of the others who joined him then pursued a second Jap, catching up with him and taking him prisoner.

While at Shuri Castle they were pinned down and held down there for several days. It was in the rain and everything else and they were just sitting there, they couldn't do anything. They had their OP set up and they were watching Shuri Castle and all the movement around there. At night when they would fire mortars we could spot them and then we'd return fire. They had their OP secured for about a week and they captured a pair of Japanese binoculars and they were very powerful. They had the glasses secured and the lenses so that they didn't reflect light during the day, very, very careful. He said they were watching for their OP's and they were watching for us. One day Swede was in the OP they were looking at the maps because the weather was beginning to change a little bit so they were thinking about making a move. The next thing they knew four Colonels and Lt. Colonels standing up on top of the ridge above them looking through their glasses. Swede looked up at them and said, "What in the hell are you doing?" The Colonel's wanted to know who he was talking to. Swede said I'm talking to you, what are you doing? They said they were getting ready to make a move. Swede said that they had better move. They said that he couldn't order them around. Swede told them to get there asses out of there right now, this is an OP and they were giving the location away. They left and didn't say more but that night they took a pounding like they never took before. They missed direct hits but they gave them an awful pounding. They stuck there because the move was being made the next day and they had to give them support. Earl got a souvenir of a Japanese sword from up there at Shuri Castle.

Earl said that the Army was off to their left and they were taking a beating and couldn't move. It seemed to be from a 105MM Howitzer. The Beach was to their right. They were getting hit with some big stuff and couldn't figure where it was at. Every day about noon it would go overhead sounding like a freight train and it was pounding the hell out of the Army. They called Swede and asked him if he could find out where it was coming from. They could hear it going over but they never bothered to find out where from because it wasn't effecting them and they didn't know it was effecting the Army. They starting looking for it and Swede would listen for the firing and time it took to go over and then hit. By that he could get a feel for distance and he came to the conclusion that it was coming from some of the small ships that they had knocked out down in the harbor. One of the ships contained an active weapon and they were firing from the deserted ship. Swede reported it in and gave them the coordinates, etc, and they sent a ship around. Earl said that he didn't know if it was the Missouri or what it was. They asked for coordinates on this and Swede said yes and gave them the coordinates and they asked for a round of smoke bursting. They said your pretty close just raise it a half a mile. When we called for artillery it was usually fifty yards or so. Swede told them that a half a mile would go clear across the island. They assured him that in a battle wagon it went in increments of a mile or half a mile. They got the right reading and they laid it right on top of them. For about five days they were knocking the hell out of the Army position.

Leaving Okinawa it was back to Puvuvu to rebuild the forces and train once again before leaving for China on September 28, 1945.

After Okinawa Earl participated in occupation of China from October 11th, 1945 to January 14th, 1946. He was stationed in Peiping China. Basically they were getting ready at that time for the invasion of Japan. They were receiving maps and information to prepare them for the ultimate invasion. Thank God for President Truman and the atom bomb, that was never needed to happen.

They left their base on China on January 14th and left the Province of China on January 19th on the Navy Transport ship USS Wakefield with 5,000 men aboard arriving at San Francisco on February 1, 1946 and leaving immediately for Chicago where he received his discharge on February 16, 1946.

His awards consisted of - Presidential Unit Citations awarded the First Marine Division, Reinforced, for services on Peleliu and on Okinawa.
Good Conduct Medal for services 1942 – 1945.
American Campaign Medal
Asiatic-Pacific Campaign Medal
China Service Medal No. 2185 for service in China 1945-1946

He got married to Ronny in 1947 and they had two children, a boy and a girl, Terrence Earl and Candace Darlene. After nineteen years the marriage ended in divorce and later he married Peggy and they have been married thirty seven years.

Friends along the way are, Richard J. Sergent, C. Edwin Yuan, H.A. Waldrop, Jr., Charles T. Ramsey, Dan W. Cass, Chester E. Carter, Edward G. Farah, Joe T. Morris, W. Louis Darby, Charles A. Linhart, Ross R. Currens, Arthur Woodcock, H. B. Rawson, Pete Westen, George C.. Lerch, Allan Boyd, George Guinn and Warren Goodwin.

Earl retired as Chief from the Middlefield, Ohio Fire Department in January, 1995.

JAMES LEE WARREN

James Lee Warren, 17620 Mayfield Road, Huntsburg
Township, Windsor, Ohio 44099

Jim was born May 20, 1936 in the old Corey Hospital in
Chardon, Ohio He was taken home by his parents Violet
and Lee Warren to the family home in North Bloomfield,
Ohio

He enrolled in Bloomfield School through the fifth grade.
His parents divorced and he went to live with his
grandparents, Clifford and Meribelle Burton in
Huntsburg, Ohio. This was temporary although it lasted
a couple of years. He attended High School in
Middlefield, Ohio through the eleventh grade and finally
moved by himself to Chardon, Ohio to finish and
graduate from Chardon High School in June of 1954.

By graduation time, Jim and two Chardon High class mates, "Red" Leggitt and Richard Ruple, had enlisted in the United States Air Force. The three went through basic training together but saw little of each other during the 13 weeks of training. Jim went to the Air Force and his High School girl friend, Eleanor Fales, went to nurses training in Cleveland.

Jim was taken to Painesville for the bus ride to Cleveland by his mother and two brothers, Fred and Bob. It was later learned that mom cried all the way home.

Jim was off on a great adventure. He left for the Air Force on June 20, 1954. After a swearing in ceremony at the Standard Building in Cleveland the whole group of enlistee's were taken a couple of blocks to the rear of what was probably a restaurant in front. They had a room in back to feed new enlistee's. Jim's first experience with 'Shit-on-a-Shingle' went just fine, he even claimed to like it. This was going to be the real McCoy now, he was in the Air Force.

From Cleveland, a quick bus ride to the airport and a one hour flight on a C-47 brought them to a rudimentary airstrip near Geneva, New York. The C-47 even had the canvas seats lined up along each wall. This was Sampson Air Force Base and his new home for the next 13 weeks.

Jim claims to have a streak of military in him that has been there since World War two. His paternal uncle, Earl Skeels, was a top turret gunner on a B-24 and was a handsome guy in his uniform. He came home on leave before going overseas. It may have been there that the "uniform" captivated Jim. Earl was another of Jim's hero's. He survived World War II but died several years later.

As a youngster, he was a school crossing guard at Huntsburg School. The position included not only responsibility but also a badge and the official belt and cross belt. The die was cast!!

As a teenager, he became active in Boy Scout Troop 97 in Middlefield, Ohio. His sense of responsibility soon won the position of patrol leader of the Beaver Patrol. And again, a uniform. His scouting abilities soon led him to the first Boy Scout Jamboree at Valley Forge, Pennsylvania. Then, President Harry S. Truman spoke to the thousands of scouts from all over the states and the world. It was the big time!! Many Scouts boarded a train for the adventure. This looked too much like a "Troop Train". Years later he found out that his mom cried the rest of the day. Jim was off on a great adventure.

The next brush with uniforms, badges, and responsibility came with an official U. S. Air Force group called the Ground Observer Corps. USAF men came to the Middlefield High School to find G.O.C. Members for a new post. Jim soon became a leader. His future wife, Eleanor, served on the same G.O.C. team. This was in 1951 or 1952. To this day, over 50 years later, Jim can still recall his post's call sign...JULIET METRO 52 RED (JM52R). The G.O.C. was a tracking system that the USAF was using to track and test new radar systems and to verify that the systems were working accurately. Once again a uniform was involved. A real Air Force man got him to join the G.O.C. and swore him in. It was Air Force all the way after that.

Basic training went well for Jim at Sampson Air Force Base. Being a country boy seemed to help as he enjoyed the food, got along OK with the hours, and even though he was not a physical marvel did get through the physical training. In later years he would comment that the end of basic was probably the last time he was in good condition. His basic training unit, Flight 3406, was pretty good over all. A couple of men (All of them were boys of 18 or 19) never did learn to march, shoot, or do all those other G.I. things but the rest covered for them and all graduated. The unit went on to the drill competition and won first place.

Basic training clothing consisted of mostly World War II clothing and equipment. The Government had warehouses full of it and it had to be used up. The one piece fatigues were "one size fits all" and Jim's crotch came down to about where his knees bent. They had to be tailored and ready for inspection at daybreak. Jim had never even sewn a button on let alone tailoring. But the job got done and some of the fellas looked weird throughout basic. The dress uniform was World War II khaki's. The fatigues were W.W.II Army Air Corps one piece type. The Air Force Blues were distributed later in basic training.

Jim never got Montezuma's revenge from the food and got along well with most of it. When liver was served, he ate what ever else was on the tray and waited for the next meal. Montezuma struck several trainees both from his unit and from others. The standing rule was to raise your hand when nature called if you were in formation. This was to excuse you for a "Nature's Call" emergency. With the revenge, time was of the essence…more than once a trainee was seen racing across the field with his arm in the air… suddenly he would screech to a stop and stand at attention….it was too late!!

The obstacle course, "camping out", the rifle range was almost a natural for a country kid. Some of the city guys had a tough time with the whole affair. The M-1 Garands and M-1 Carbines being used on the training range were very well used and had little accuracy left in them. If you could manage to hit the general target area, it was called a "hit". They were told by their grizzled range Sergeant that "if the enemy gets too close, throw the damned thing at them and run like hell". It isn't likely that ever happened.

After basic, and a series of tests, Jim was offered several fields in which to get further training. Those who scored less than good were sent to a variety of USAF bases for "on-the-job-training (ojt)". At least Jim had some choice in his future. Jim chose to go into the medical field as he had driven ambulance for a funeral home and a doctor before the service. He said that no one had medical training on ambulances in those days. It was more of a "swoop and scoop" job then.

Jim was accepted into the field and was promptly assigned to the U. S. Army For Combat Medic School at the 4th Army Medical Center at <u>Fort Sam Houston,</u> San Antonio, Texas. Training went very well and Jim graduated near the top of a group that held over 150 Army and Air Force Medics.

From Fort Sam Houston, he spent a few days at San Marco, Texas riding around in helicopters. It was just a "try-it-and-see-if-you-like-it" exercise.

From San Marcos, Jim got his first leave and was to proceed to Fairchild Air Force Base near Spokane, Washington. Spokane was to leave a long standing love affair with the Pacific Northwest. His leave was short. Said "Hi" to mom, saw his girlfriend, Eleanor, and said Hi to his poor civilian friends. Jim's mom again said that he really didn't go into the service, only that he was off on another grand adventure.

Then off to Spokane and adventure Part II. He and others arrived in Spokane by train in the middle of the night and had to call for a Fairchild Air Force Base pick-up bus. It was promised to be there in a few minutes. The bus finally arrived about day break. They still had to report to the base Commander within 15 minutes of their arrival. They were a scruffy looking bunch by then. They looked rough after 3 or 4 days on a troop train. Some of them might have been a little drunk.

The base shuttle bus finally picked Jim up and after another hour of riding around the base finally delivered him to the hospital compound. It was a very old World War II era wooden barracks. It had a statue of a Greek God (Mercury) with wings and a tin hat on it out front. The statue was fairly complete anatomically and suffered numerous embarrassing attachments periodically. The hospital Commander would go crazy every time the statue was adorned as the nurses, the public, and everyone in between went past it to get into the hospital. The "enlisted swine" usually saluted the adorned statue upon entering the hospital as the decorations were just beautiful.

His first assignment was with the 99th Heavy Reconnaissance (Recon) Group of the 15th Air Force. The hospital unit was part of the 99th. He found out that the 99th was scheduled to go to Guam shortly and on to Westover AFB in Massachusetts later on. Jim got out of that by buying another airman, Pete Sicilian, who had the same qualifications, a bottle of good scotch.

He was then transferred to the 92nd Heavy Bombardment Group that was a part of the <u>Strategic Air Command.</u> He was then in the 92nd Tactical Hospital Group.

Because of Jim's training, and test scores, he was assigned to the surgical unit. This turned out to be a somewhat elite group as most medics were assigned to other jobs. Surgery turned out to be Jim's forte. He learned quickly and was soon put in charge of a shift. A second and third stripe came along without further testing.

Another opening came along that fit better in with his job and his medical training. The Fairchild Helicopter Air & Sea Rescue Team needed people due to discharges, etc. Jim had played with helicopters in San Marcos, Texas in 1954 and was qualified to start more training. Jets had not come along as yet and the Post-Korean War "H-19" choppers were still being used. Not all of them had crashed in Korea. The H-19 had a 19 cylinder rotary engine in the nose of the craft. When it quit humming, it became nose heavy and soon after became a falling rock. Jim's story about Korea wasn't published.

The rescue team did considerable training and made a few rescues before Jim's discharge. One rescue effort sent them out into the mountains to extract an airman who had ridden a motorcycle over into a ravine. The guy had been there trapped under the motorcycle for two or three days. A civilian hunter found him. With no where to land, Jim was lowered by cable to start rescue proceedings. Training paid off and the guy was removed to surgery at Fairchild AFB. The extended time in the wild resulted in a severe case of gas gangrene...a very odorous problem requiring a strong stomach to be around. The airman had to go through two amputations before the surgeons could get ahead of the gas gangrene. Months later, the airman went home on a medical discharge. Before leaving, he came in and thanked the whole rescue team and the hospital staff.

Because of Jim's flying status and something else the Air Force had in mind, Jim was put through a ridged investigation both of his records and his neighbors and family at home. It scared hell out of the neighbors and his mom. They thought Jim has gotten into some kind of deep trouble. In fact, Jim was getting a high security clearance. Jim said he even had clearance for rumors!!!

With this security clearance, and the ever present "Russian threat" on the DEW (Distant Early Warning) Line, the air-sea rescue team would occasionally take off in the late evening, fly to a mountain top or radar base and pick up someone dressed in civilian clothes. He often had a briefcase handcuffed to him and he totally lacked social skills...He wouldn't speak to the crew.

Someone would close the hatch and the chopper would take off. This person would then be flown to somewhere else and dropped off for another crew to pick up and go on. One such trip dropped a guy off over in Montana. Ya gotta love the cloak and dagger stuff.

The chopper team wasn't a large part of Jim's day because they were not near the ocean and there were three teams so his name didn't come up that often. As a postmark, three or four months after Jim was discharged and back home, his chopper crew crashed and all were killed. It was definitely time to go home!!!

Most rescues on the huge base came from mishaps on the flight line. Shortly after arriving at Fairchild, a B-36 crashed and killed all but the tail gunner. The TG got out almost un-scratched. Being the new guy, Jim, and others, had to go out and scrape up enough toes and thumbs to have a decent burial.

After about two years of service, Jim went before the hospital Commander and requested permission to marry his High School girl friend, Miss Eleanor Rae Fales and to go on leave to get married. It was a very nervous time as he wasn't sure what all marriage entailed and it was also the first time he had ever reported directly to the Commander. All went well though and Jim rode to Minneapolis, Minnesota with a good friend and took a bus the rest of the way to Chardon, Ohio arriving at two o'clock in the morning. The Chardon policeman, Chief

John Bowles, picked him up, and because he was a service man took him home to Middlefield. John is gone now but Jim holds a soft spot for him in his heart.

Before getting married, servicemen had to go before the Commander to request permission to be married. The USAF required this to keep someone from going out and getting drunk and coming home with some floozy he wanted to marry. It also kept control over the spousal money given once married. Jim's pay went from $107.00 per month to $152.00 once married.

A beautiful wedding at the family farm in Huntsburg was followed by a very short honeymoon. Jim & Eleanor joined for another adventure that at the time of this writing has lasted over 48 years. The train trip back to Spokane again got them into Spokane in the middle of the night. His Captain was away on leave and had given Jim her home for two weeks in which to get acclimated. The Captain had tied bells to the bed springs under the bed and had removed the bolts holding the bed down. A rather noisy reception, according to Jim.

By the time an airman was a qualified surgical specialist, he had gone through several filtering processes. Some were to receive further surgical training and others went to other duties both in the hospital and in other outside medical fields. Jim's group was a top notch and well trained group. In later years, the 92nd Tactical Hospital (Jim's unit) of the Strategic Air Command produced two medical doctors, at least one pharmacist, a dentist, two registered nurses, two independent medics (previous to there being paramedics), and Dave Vorpahl who holds a Bachelors Degree, two masters degrees (in Biology and adult education), and a PhD in Adult Education. Oh yes, Vorpahl also became a Certified Cytologist and a Medical Technologist along the way. One other buddy made the big time too..."Tiny" Arthur Greer, became a Taxi Driver who ran a taxi business and moonshine running business in South Carolina. The group was not to be trifled with. Jim stays in touch with several of his best buddies.

The 92nd Tactical Hospital was designed as a Regional Hospital, as well as a Tactical Field Hospital complete with dental, orthopedic, surgery, recovery, and the associated mess halls and quarters just like in the movie and TV series M.A.S.H.... It was a large undertaking that had to be set up at least for practice every year. It was a huge job. It was literally a canvas and wood frame city.

Prior to marriage, Jim lived in the old World War II wooden barracks that were paper thin. The Spokane weather in winter can include several feet of snow and several degrees below zero temperatures. Jim said his first barracks had signs in it warning them not to shoot Indians from the windows. The old barracks had enough gaps and holes to place small snow drifts beside the bunks. One man "Buster Barube" had as his only duty the coal firing and maintenance of several barracks heating systems.

Base "Alerts" were pretty common in the era of the Russian Bear. Alerts were accompanied by an awful sounding "Klaxon" on the flight line and large erie sounding sirens for the rest of the base. If you were on base, you had minutes to be at your duty station. If you were authorized to be in town, you had a maximum of one-half hour to report. It was about 15 miles from the base to Spokane and you didn't want to be on the road when the alert sounded. World speed records were set on the main highway. Jim was never late!!

Jim is a member of the <u>Society of the Strategic Air Command.</u> The Society puts out a newsletter called "The Klaxon". It was a serious part of the Air Force life. The 92nd was a part of the <u>Strategic Air Command</u> and in turn a part of the Distant Early Warning System (DEW LINE). As such, everyone was convinced that the Russians would come over the top of the world and come right down our throats. Fairchild AFB was a nuclear base with the largest bombers in the world. At first, the base had the monstrous B-36. Towards the end of Jim's enlistment, the equally large B-52's were coming in. Either bomber precluded sleep for Jim as his barracks was near the last two-thirds of the runway and the planes were really pouring on the coal to take off. This went on day and night as SAC always had command ships aloft at any given time. They had no intention of getting caught by the Russians. Those were jittery times. Jim Claims he has never seen a Russian.

The B-36 Bomber had six "Pusher" engines and four outboard jets. It had unbelievable power and pretty loud when taking off. One had to pull themselves through a tunnel to get from one section to another. No place for claustrophobia.

One of the off-shoots of the regular base alerts and DEW LINE warnings was that Jim's wife and small group of other wives had a "Plan B". In the event that the world did come apart, the wives were to go to a specified cabin at Lake Sasheen well up in the mountains of Eastern Washington State. Lake Sasheen was 2 or 3 hours away from Fairchild AFB and could be gotten to without going through Spokane. The cabin belonged to Jim's Captain, Vera B. Lee.

Capt. Lee stayed on and eventually retired from the Air Force as a Lt. Colonel. Jim still has the "Colton Banana Distributors" wooden box that the emergency supplies were kept in. All survivors of the group were to meet at Sasheen as soon as they could.

Captain Lee (retired as a Lt. Colonel) died in the summer of 2003. She always had the respect of all who served under her...she entered the military as a nurse in the World War II Army Air Corps. She stayed in contact with dozens of her Air Force family all of her years.

Jim's first child, son "Gary Lee" was born in 1956 at the Fairchild Air Force Hospital, an Air Force brat. Gary grew up to be a professional fireman. He was a Lieutenant in the East Cleveland Fire Department for 19 years and is currently a Captain in the Murphy Fire Department, Murphy, Texas.

Jim and Eleanor drove back to Ohio to let the family see the new addition. The leave went well but on the return trip the weather turned out bad and a Southern route had to be taken around the mountains. Brother Fred went along to help drive. The Southern route had its problems too. A sand storm put them a day or so behind schedule. Jim contacted the American Red Cross who contacted Fairchild AFB so that he would not be AWOL. It worked out well but the Air Force added two more days to his enlistment.

Jim made "Buck Sergeant" (Airman First Class – a three striper) in his third year of service. He never concentrated on getting rank as he was happy with the job, his marriage, and the way his life was going. He didn't even dream of "Getting Out" as most other G.I.'s do. Jim took every class or school that was made available to him. All of this had to fit in with his regular job in surgery. The surgical staff took turns at being on 24 hour call.

Schedule notwithstanding, Jim went through, and graduated from the high altitude chamber required of all air crews. A friend in his former barracks, Bill Wolfington "Wolf", worked in the chamber and smoothed the way. The chamber is like a large bathysphere tank where the internal pressures can simulate high altitude conditions. To graduate one had to be taken to 100,000 feet and learn how to survive. After 10,000 feet, oxygen is required. After 12,000 feet, if not supported, you quietly go to sleep. If an attendant doesn't intervene with oxygen, it's all over very peacefully. Another qualification was to survive a "Rapid Decompression" as might occur with a sudden breach of a pressurized aircraft such as a bullet hit or some other sudden change in pressure. Some fun!!

An opening in the newly forming base honor guard and drill team caught Jim's attention. He had been on an "Honor" flight in basic training and thought he could march. His Captain gave the blessing to join the team as long as other duties were not neglected. The Drill Instructor turned out to be a former Marine with marching in mind. Most everything Jim knew had to be relearned this new Sergeants way. The end result was an honor guard and drill team that was in great demand. They didn't miss any of the parades for miles around and they preceded all Fairchild Air Force Base functions.

One highlight was when SAC Commander, General Curtis E. Lemay, came to inspect Fairchild Air Force

Base. The team stood honor guard as the General got off the plane. Lemay had a reputation for being a tough guy that went back to World War II. He exited the plane with his ever present cigar in his mouth. A big no-no on the flight line. Some poor Air Policeman approached him and asked the General as politely as possible to remove the cigar. The cigar had to go. Otherwise, the whole area (laden with fuels, fumes, etc.) might blow the place up. General Lemays reply was..."it wouldn't dare". The young AP took silence as his best defense. The General then proceeded to pull tee-shirt collars out of every third man on the drill team to see if the shirt was clean. He knew they were clean...he just wanted everyone to know that he was there and that he was in charge. Later, each drill team member and the air policeman received a congratulatory letter from the General.

The former Marine drill instructor had done his job. He soon transferred to another base....probably to terrorize another bunch of guys dumb enough to sign up for a new team. Before he left, Jim's team was able to do an excellent "Queen Anne's Salute"...a complicated maneuver. With bayonets installed, it had to be done without filleting the man in front of you.

The Strategic Air Command, being a nuclear armed command, was very tight on security. There were stories of airmen being shot when they were challenged. They would panic and run rather than have to explain why they were where they were. The air police had the authority to do what they had to do to stop what might have been a foreign agent or a saboteur.

Along with the tight security, a badge had to be shown to get on the flight line and you had to have a reason to be there. It was great sport to glue a picture of a monkey or one of the three stooges on your badge and see if it gained you access. It would work for a while and then the AP's raised hell with you. Some of the funny ID's worked for weeks. The AP's didn't do much other than a good tail chewing. They were too embarrassed that you had pulled it off for so long.

Jim gave some thought to staying in the Air Force but decided against it mainly for family reasons. Both Jim's and Eleanor's family were back in Ohio

During his continuation in the Air Force Reserves he was promoted to Staff Sergeant.

Jim's medical, surgical training in the U.S. Air Force held him in good stead in his civilian endeavors. He made good use of his medical, surgical assistant training in the Geauga County Hospitals and as a volunteer Rescue Captain with the Burton, Ohio Fire Department for 28 years. Jim used his military training as a part time Deputy and Dispatcher for the Geauga County sheriffs Department for 14 years.

Jim went to the Kent State University under the G.I. Bill for two years.

Jim and Eleanor were blessed with two more children. A daughter born in 1958, Debra Rae. Debra and her husband have two stores for a costume and magic business. Another son was born in 1961, David James who works in the plastic field and does machine repair and maintenance for a large plastic injection molding company in Middlefield, Ohio

Jim credits the Air Force with instilling self confidence, responsibility and flexibility in whatever circumstances come along. He says a good sense of humor is an asset as there are times when something humorous must be found in pretty bad situations. A good sense of humor keeps you alive and interested...and he says, ready for the next adventure!!

Jim's medals and citations are:
National Defense Service Medal
US Army Good Conduct Medal
US Air Force Good Conduct Medal
Presidential Unit Citation with Two Oak Leaves
Surgical Unit Citation for Life Saving

The Army Good Conduct probably came from the time spent with the Army's 4th Army Medical Center, Fort Sam Houston, San Antonio, Texas. Never figured that one out but that's what they issued. The Presidential

Unit Award was from the Berlin Airlift days long before Jim's service time. The 99th and the 92nd had both been involved. During World War II, the 15th Air Force flew mainly out of Foggia, Italy. The 15th Air Force was making the raids on the Ploesti Oil Fields and later flew stripped down bombers in the rescue of airman and other prisoners from a German prison camp late in the war.

Two more commemorative medals have recently been authorized: The Cold War Recognition Medal, and the US Air Force Service Medal. Neither of these are considered "earned" medals but nice to have.

Jim is now semi-retired and lives with Eleanor in a beautiful log home in Huntsburg, Ohio. Still works part time. He says that too much time on his hands causes him to want to travel again. His 9 grand children help keep him busy.

Jim is very active in the Atwood-Mauck American Legion Post 459 in Burton, Ohio. He has served as the Post Adjutant for several years and enjoys it very much

He also serves as the Atwood-Mauck Corporation Post 459 Secretary/Treasurer.

A few years ago he joined the Sampson Air Force Base Veterans Association. He also belongs to the Society of the Strategic Air Command.

Like most Veterans, the training and respect never completely leaves your life. Jim says he doesn't want it to.

Go SAC!!.....Go Air Force!!

Jim's mother, Violet, and her friend "Teeter" Grosvenor, have traveled several states and have published four books on Geauga County Veterans genealogy together. Both women are considered authorities on Veterans genealogical subjects. Violet's research has led her and another friend, Stella Chandler, to England, Ireland, Wales, Scotland and a little bit of Germany. There are few cemeteries and libraries left untouched. "Teeter" and Violet have researched many records and have found every Veteran in the Geauga County area ranging from the Revolutionary War times through the Korean War. Violet is now 91 years old and still works on the computer. It is through some of this background that Jim has learned his respect and admiration for America and its Veterans. He became a Patriot.

LT. COL. CYNTHIA ANN WONG

Cynthia Ann Wong, 11787 Bell Road, Newbury, Ohio 44065-9582

Born Cynthia Ann Olson in Barre, Vermont, January 3rd, 1962.

Cynthia's dad, Thomas William Olson, is a Korean War Veteran as is her uncle, Conrad Olson. These are the only members of her immediate family who served in the military.

Cynthia graduated from Concord High in Wilmington, Delaware in 1980 and the University of Delaware in 1984 with a major in English Education. She worked as technical writer for ten years and a public relation specialist for another two years. She is currently a full-time parent with two small children. Cynthia is a Lt.Colonel in the Air Force Reserve and has been the

Mission Support Flight Commander for going on seven years.

Cynthia joined the military July 5, 1979 at the age of seventeen. She went to Basic training at Ford Jackson, South Carolina three days after she graduated from High school. She stayed in the same barracks as her dad had before her some 30 years previous and was part of one of the first companies to have integrated male and females with one platoon of females and three platoons of males. Her platoon started out with fifty women and ended up graduating thirty-five because of the strenuous physical training.

Cynthia started her enlistment as a track vehicle mechanic in the Delaware Army Guard to learn something about the workings of her car. The guard had a program called a split option where she went to basic training one summer and completed her technical education at Aberdeen Proving Grounds, Maryland for the following summer. She was a member of the 262 Heavy Equipment Maintenance Company out of Delaware City for about five years. She enjoyed being a mechanic, but it was boring because there was not enough to do. She would find jobs to keep busy. She reorganized the technical publication library and the shop van and filed papers in the orderly room. Her willingness to go beyond was recognized, resulting in her early promotion to E-5.

Before her enlistment was completed, a senior NCO spoke with Cynthia and persuaded her to re-enlist. She decided to retrain in to another career field, eventually applying for the Delaware Guard's Officer Training Program, which was 13 months of pure hell. In 1986 Cynthia was commissioned a 2nd Lieutenant in the Aviation Branch.

Cynthia joined the aviation branch primarily because she had heard the pilots lived pretty will. Never mind that she had a fear of heights. She went to flight school in 1987 and graduated in 1988.

Cynthia was the last small person to go through flight school because the anthropometric standards had changed for arm length and leg length to accommodate new aircraft. She got a waiver to attend flight school. She was a member of one of the last classes that flew the TH-55 at Fort Rucker, Alabama, the home of Army Aviation. Initially, all students went through the TH-55 course, where they teach all about the mechanics of the Helicopter. The TH-55 is a two-seater that can be flown with the doors off. The first time she soloed, she could barely land the aircraft. By the end of flight school she had gotten rid of her fear of heights.

While she was in flight school, Cynthia met her future husband Tezeon Wong through a mutual friend. They dated for six months and became engaged shortly before Tezeon was stationed in Korea for a year. When she finished flight school, she went back to the Delaware Guard Unit to fly. She hauled supplies and people; she even did some formation flying.

When Tezeon got back from Korea, he got out of the service and Cynthia and Tezeon were married September 23, 1989. Tezeon accepted a job in Cleveland, Ohio. The year they moved to Ohio, the Persion Gulf War started. Cynthia transferred to a Medevac Unit; the Lorain County 316th Medical Evacuation Detachment. She did some flying with them and was living in Eastlake for a couple of months. She and her husband purchased a home in Newbury in October 1990. The month after they moved into the house, Cynthia was activated to go to war. Cynthia was actually in Saudi Arabia and Iraq longer that she had been in Ohio.

The first part of the activation was at Fort Knox, Kentucky where the unit helicopters were converted from H to "Victor" models. Special coatings had to be applied to the rotors to prevent damage from sand erosion. The unit spent Christmas at Fort Knox. Every minute that her husband could get away, he would come down to Fort Knox to be with her. The unit spent about a month at Fort Knox and then left for Southwest Asia on Cynthia's birthday January 3, 1991.

They took off to Westover Air Force Base, Massachusetts to refuel and pickup additional personnel. This was the point of debarkation for all flight going out of the country. Westover AFB was a wonderful facility that catered to military people coming and going. After a short stop at Westover, the unit was flown to Moron AFB Spain and received the same kind of Air Force treatment as Westover: Red Cross Volunteers greeted them, they had a beautiful hanger set up with cots with provisions for them to take showers, and hot coffee, - and it was wonderful.

After an 8-hour delay at Moron AFB, the unit arrived at Dhahran Airport three o'clock in the morning. The unit boarded a bus and waited two hours until billeting could be located for them at the port. With flashlights that they had brought with them, the unit located some floor space in the warehouse to grab a few hours of sleep. In the morning, Cynthia woke up with five hundred to a thousand people sharing the same accommodations with her in the warehouse. Everyone was waiting for his or her equipment to arrive by boat. There were homemade port-a-johns outside, overflowing with human waste; it was literally an open sewer and the smell was horrid. Cynthia saw Colonels washing their own laundry out of plastic tubs—close by the warehouse. It looked like a third world country.

The next morning the unit Commander, Major Ernie Hollo and First Sergeant Jim Davidson attempted to locate the unit that they were supposed to join in the combat zone. Unfortunately, the primary unit had departed to an unknown location somewhere north in the neutral zone. It would take a short time for the unit to gather its equipment and put the helicopters back together to locate the unit up north.

First Sergeant Davidson relocated the unit to Khobar Towers. Khobar Towers are seven to eight floor high-rise apartments that the Saudi government had built in an attempt to colonize the Bedouins. The project failed and the apartments were vacant for ten years. When the Persian Gulf War started, the Saudi government allowed the Americans to house their military in the complex. The beautiful apartments were decorated with mahogany woodwork, plush carpets, and gold bathroom fixtures. Forty people shared a three-bedroom apartment that was designed for a family of five.

There were literally thousand of people living in Khobar Towers, which was a flagrant violation of force protection—never concentrate the troops so the enemy could easily destroy them. There were other problems involved in putting such a large amount of people in such a concentrated area. Sanitation was a huge problem and because Americans are so wasteful they literally sucked the local Saudi town dry of water. The town shut the water off so there was no water to flush toilets or to take showers. Cynthia's unit had to wash with bottled water and whatever water they could tank in with purification tablets. Military members had to decide when they got their ration of six bottles of water, whether to wash or to have something to drink.

The huge vacant parking garages were set up as chow halls and the cooks were Pakistan civilian, hired by the military to feed the troops. Cynthia remembers it as the worst food she had ever eaten in her life. She remembers having to stand in line for an hour and the joke was that once you ate, it was time to stand in the line for the next meal.

Cynthia was a pilot and the designated supply officer. Military finance gave her five thousand dollars to spend on items that the unit needed such as TVs, carpet, heaters or anything that would make their life more comfortable. She purchased generators so they could have electricity and heaters.

A couple of times she got the chance to shop at a western grocery store. In full combat gear, Cynthia shopped among all these women in their full-length black religious coverings. Cynthia had a loaded weapon in the seat of the basket with her gas mask. She would go down the aisle and the women would clear the aisles to avoid her. In addition to buying things for the unit, she bought cigarettes and cereal for some of her comrades that had given her personal money to buy things for them.

Military Intelligence was poorly conveyed during and after the war. Her unit was unable to obtain meaningful and timely information. Therefore, like the rest of the

United States, she and her comrades resorted to watching news accounts on CNN. Here is a funny example of how people figured out what was happening through other situations. After about a week all the military folks were served a nice meal compared to the garbage that they usually got. They were served steaks, potato, salad, apple pie, near beer, the non-alcoholic beer. Many of her fellow unit members joked around saying, do you get the feeling like this is your last supper or something? Sure enough one o'clock when they were watching CNN along with the rest of the United States, the air war started. They watched all the reporters donning gas masks. They watched the scuds being launched from Iraq heading towards Khobar Towers, which was where the unit was living. Everybody got into full MOP gear and there was utter chaos as people in the upper floors evacuated to lower levels. They had to wear their MOP suits for a very long time, which was absolute torture for the unit chain smokers. Some smokers needed a cigarette and took their masks off to smoke outside. They witnessed the Patriot intercepting the Scud. There was some debris, but they did not have any chemical or biological weapons on them.

The next morning the unit decided to head north towards Iraq to locate their mother unit. They took their helicopters first and the vehicles followed in a convoy with another larger group. One of the warrant officers, who was a Pennsylvania State Cop, was frustrated by the slow pace of following a hundred other trucks and tanks and made the decision to break from the main convoy. There is a story that the breakaway convoy actually missed a turn and headed by accident to Kuwait. They knew something was wrong when they could actually see the fire bombing taking place around them. Fortunately, they did a U-turn and were able to get back on the right way to find the other people in the unit who had flown up with the helicopters.

The 316th's mission was to support the medical companies of the 1st CAV. Cynthia was with "Charlie" Medical Company; they divided the crews and they actually stayed up north in the neutral zone with the medical company HQs personnel. The unit was positioned very close to a medical supply battalion and majority of the unit members actually lived on a garbage dump. The local rulers of Hafr Albatin wanted to minimize contact with the Americans so they positioned most of the military units well outside the towns. Many of the troops were concerned about the threat of anthrax from the garbage dump more that the scuds dispersing it.

Each Helicopter crew consisted of a pilot, co-pilot, crew chief and an EMT. They were positioned with medical companies for medical evacuation. Because the terrain was difficult to travel by motor vehicle, helicopters were routinely used to transport individuals around to various areas. Helicopters were the quickest and best way to get around. Cynthia's most dangerous mission was to pick a General Officer up on the front lines that had a dental emergency. For this war, more people were killed by accidents than combat. Many intelligence reports predicted mass casualties due to chemical and biological weapons. Cynthia believes that the prayers and support of the American people avoided the loss in casualties. The prayers and letters they received helped the morale of the unit members. People were also incredibly generous with sending food and personal items.

For the most part, the war was very boring so boring that Cynthia was able to read the novel 'War and Peace' in about four weeks. She quoted a piece that she recalled hearing, 'That war is a long moment of shear boredom punctuated by moments of shear terror.' That's what it was for them. Cynthia had one aircraft emergency when she was in Iraq and both she and the pilot were able to land the aircraft safely without any further damage. Cynthia was also involved with evacuating casualties from the front medical units to the rear areas.

Cynthia had some good and bad experiences with the local Saudis because she was a female. The religious Moslems spit on her while she was in uniform. Some of the Western educated Saudi men were very respectful and gave her some gifts through the male soldiers. Out of respect, they did not speak to her directly as is custom in their country.

Cynthia said that the unit had fun improving their food situation by finding and making their own cooking equipment to save them from having to go somewhere else to eat. Those with cooking skill signed up to make gourmet meals out of canned items and whatever else the unit was able to get at a local market. There was a movie tent set up for nightly entertainment. There was a volleyball court set up and the unit had civil engineers assist them in digging a swimming pool that eventually got national coverage.

The trip back to the United States was wonderful. United Airlines took them back in style and had the whole plane decorated with artwork from kids. The plane landed in Westover Air Force Base and they literally got the red carpet treatment. Every high-ranking officer from Westover met them as they disembarked the plane. The hangar had a band, free beer, hot dogs, and many American Flags. The legend being told is that the local people of Westover took a sacred responsibility to meet every airplane that came back into the country to their Airbase. They met every plane with the same welcome, no matter how late at night. The local veterans always came out to the welcome back party. There were Veterans from WWII, Korea, Vietnam all meeting at the end of the red carpet. They shook their hands and welcomed them home. Her unit had many Vietnam Vets who openly wept at this amazing reception, a painful reminder of the one that they never did receive coming back from a different war.

The unit flew from Westover AFB to Fort Knox for a week and then anti-climatically, a charter bus drove the unit back to their unit in Lorain County. Along the way as they hit Ohio, there were flags, yellow ribbons, and many signs. Cynthia could not believe the welcome home that they received. It is something that she will never forget. Many unit members left the service upon returning and there was a high divorce rate within her unit—30%. Some unit members came down with the Persian Gulf Syndrome.

Cynthia said that when she got back from Iraq that she transferred to the Air Force Reserve. Her husband stayed in the Army Reserve and flew with 316th Medevac unit for a couple of years. The 316th Medevac detachment disbanded in 1995. Cynthia said that she still keeps in touch with some of the members of the former 316th Medevac detachment. Everyone is doing well and many have retired and are doing fun things like being involved with the local American Legion.

Cynthia still keeps quite busy with her two children and her membership in the Burton, Ohio American Legion Post 459, the Newbury, Ohio VFW Post 1068 and various neighborhood, school and church functions. That is when she isn't performing her periodical functions as a Lt. Col. In the Air Force Reserves.

LT. COL. TEZEON YORKCHOUNG WONG

Tezeon Y. Wong, 11787 Bell Road, Newbury, Ohio 44065-9582

Born June 6, 1958 in New York City to Man Ping and Helga Wong.

Graduated from Middletown Senior High School, Middletown, New York in 1976

After high school, Tezeon and a friend from talked about joining the military services. His friend wanted to join the Marine Corp and Tezeon talked about joining the Army to travel the world and ride motorcycles. He heard that the Army was using motorcycles for reconnaissance at Fort Hood Texas. On the 23rd of November 1976, he enlisted in Newark, New Jersey and left for training at Fort Knox, Kentucky. They offered him a chance to go to Fort Dix for basic training, but he never had an opportunity to travel much as a kid so he chose Fort Knox instead. He did his basic and AIT

(Advanced Individual Training) together at Fort Knox. He enlisted originally for four years as an Army Reconnaissance Scout, which was Eleven Delta and is now Nineteen Delta, MOS (Military Occupational Specialty). He learned how to do scouting, radio procedures, some demolition work, how to report out, shot some of the more advanced weapons and learned to do some cavalry operations using the M113 armored personnel carrier.

From Ft. Knox he went to Fort Hood, Texas for his first duty station. While he was there he received orders to go to West Point Prep School. He was at Fort Hood from March, 1977 to June 1977 when he got orders to turn in to the Prep School that July. It was for enlisted personnel that scored high enough on their entrance examine to brush up on their academics and school work for appointment to West Point. He attended West Point from the summer of 1978, reported in July as a new Cadet, and was inducted into the class of 1982. He graduated as a Second Lieutenant.

From West Point he went to the Airborne School at Fort Benning, Georgia. That summer he reported back to Fort Knox, Kentucky for Cavalry Officer basic course. He had orders at that time for flight school, he was accepted to Army Aviation Flight School. He went down to Fort Rucker, Alabama that late fall, to report in for flight school. He got out of the Army Flight School in late 1983.

He then went to the Cobra transition, age one Cobra transition, and reported in as Hawaii's Cobra Pilot by March of 1984. Spent three years there flying Cobra's and doing attack helicopter tactics. He had a chance to see a lot of the Hawaiian Islands. He was deployed to Japan one time, to Korea a couple of times for exercises and just had a great time flying Army Helicopters.

After eighteen months from graduating from the Academy he was promoted to First Lieutenant. In 1986 he was promoted to Captain and was a Captain until 1994 when he got out of the Reserves. He got off of active duty in 1990 after he did a tour of three years in Hawaii and went back to Fort Rucker for advance course, or refresher course, in aviation maintenance officers course. He finished that off at Fort Eustis, Virginia. In the period of the advance course is when he met Cynthia, his wife, who was also going to flight school. She became a Huey Pilot, for the Delaware National Guard at the time. He then went to Korea after aviation maintenance course and spent a year there from March 14, 1988 to March 14, 1989. Came back to the states and spent a year at Savannah, Georgia where he got off of active duty. At that time frame he was a maintenance officer. During the year he was at Savannah, Georgia he was with the 24th Infantry Division. If had had stayed on active duty for another four or five months he would have gone over with them to Saudi Arabia for the Desert Storm, Desert Shield operation.

At present he is a Command and General Staff Instructor here in the Reserves. He teaches in either Cleveland or Akron. Headquarters is located in Columbus, Ohio. The 1284 CGSC Battalion is headquartered in Columbus. They teach in various locations depending where the students come from. The students are either National Guard or Reserve Majors who need to continue on with their Military education to be eligible for promotion to Lieutenant Colonel. Every once in a while they get active duty personnel to come through. Tezeon is presently a Lieutenant Colonel. The training he does covers Staff Operations at the Brigade and Division level. Also how to become a better Staff Officer at logistical planning, understand combined arms operations, fire support, air support, logistics, intelligence, coordination, sustainment, operations, personnel replacement in other words they discuss the entire scope of operations at the operational level of warfare. Not so much talking about moving platoons, companies or battalions around but talking more about how to sustain operations in division and higher Corp level. Due to the fact it is all classroom activity he is able to work out of his home with all, at present, classroom activity in Akron, Ohio. His schedule is like regular Reservists, one week end a month. He also goes two weeks AT (Annual Tour) to Fort Dix, New Jersey. Part of their schooling when they have the students show up for two weeks, after they have them for the full year when they show up for class once a month then they go to a two week faze where they go through actual staff planning exercises with them. That's their actual two week annual tour then they go back prepping for the next teaching cycle.

Tezeon is attending the U. S. Army War College presently and is about half way through right now. He said that he goes into his first two week faze in a couple of weeks. It will be at the Carlisle Barracks, Pennsylvania. Going through this will put him in a competitive position for rank of full Colonel. He presently has twenty two years in towards retirement and his MRD (Mandatory Retirement Date) is the year 2010.

He married Cynthia Ann Olson in September 23, 1989

They have two children a girl and a boy.

His medals consist of the Good Conduct Medal, Several Army Achievement Medals, Two Overseas Ribbons, one for Hawaii and one for Korea and an Army Service Ribbon, Parachutist Badge, Air Assault Badge and Army Aviator Badge.

He belongs to Quad A which is American Army Aviation Assoc. which is an Association for Army Helicopter Pilots. He belongs to ROA (Reserve Officers Assoc.), MOA (Military Officers Assoc.) the Air Force Assoc., and the Veterans of Foreign Wars.

He said that he has met a lot of good and interesting people along the way. He has enjoyed a lot of good travel, to Germany, the Far East, Korea, Hawaii and a good part of the United States.

He says that he would certainly encourage any High School kid to join the services. It will help you to decide what you want to do in life and teaches you a little discipline and definitely teaches you how to make the most of your time and your life. 'Be All You Can Be' is more than just a slogan.

He still keeps in contact with a couple from the Academy and gets together at all the reunions. An Alumni association that gets together every five years at the Academy.

He hasn't flown a helicopter since 1996 since the 316th stood down and retired their colors. They turned their helicopters over to the National Guard. Now he flies fixed wing every once in a while to stay current. He flies out of the Lorain, Ohio Airport in small Cessna's.

Tezeon got called in to active duty and left on October 23, 2004. The purpose of his activation is to train Iragi soldiers. They said that his recall will be for twelve to eighteen months. His first move was to Camp Atterbury, Indiana for briefing and training until November 29. He was then flown to Kuwait for additional training for one or two weeks.

Tezeon and his fellow men have run into some difficulty on obtaining some supplies and equipment that they discovered that they would have to provide out of their own pockets. It's a very disconcerting problem that Cynthia, his wife, is making a congressional inquiry. All that became aware of the problem is quite concerned and is following up on it.

Tezeon has been selected to head a team of seven to provide advise and guidance to an Iraqi Brigade.

GREGORY ALAN WORKMAN

Gregory A. Workman, 333 Apt. 1, West Park Avenue, Niles, Ohio 44448

Born May 4, 1971 in Champion, Ohio and grew up in Cortland.

He attended Mathews High School in Vienna, Ohio and dropped out in his senior year with two credits short to receive his diploma.

The day his class graduated was his first day in boot camp on June 2, 1989. He attended boot camp at the Great Lakes Naval Station at Chicago, Illinois. After Boot Camp he was sent to Orlando, Florida where he received training in Quartermaster "A" school, Navigational Piloting and Meteorological Observer. He said that he learned navigation and even navigating by the stars. Greg said that one time when coming back from the North Atlantic they turned off all their sophisticated satellite navigation equipment and made the return trip by the stars and the sun with the old Sextant. Upon reaching the point where they had to turn on their satellite equipment they found that they were within three hundred yards.

Next he was assigned to Norfolk, Virginia Navy yard and was there one day and he was gone for six and a half months. He boarded the Yorktown a Ticonderoga Class guided missile cruiser. They went to the Mediterranean and the first port he hit was Palma, Spain on the island of Mallorca. They were there four days and they took in the sights. Half the island was like a castle and a fort which seemed to have been originally to guard entrances to Spain. Now it is a tourist attraction for European holidays. He said that it was a beautiful place but could have been a little bit cleaner. Incredible architecture and statues

They next went to Roda Spain, a navy base but he never went off the base. They were just there for about a day and a half, just to refuel, etc.

Next they went to Cartagena and spent four days there. In Cartagena they arrived there a couple of weeks after they had a huge mud slide. It did a lot of damage. They had a program aboard ship where they would accumulate funds and when they hit a port and the town was in need they would go out and help rebuild things, they would help rebuild homes, repair things and help clean up as well as give out some money. They would also interact with the locals in some sports, such as soccer and as he said they usually got their butt kicked. Considering what had happened to the town it was very nice with all cobble stone streets and statues. The work they did to help was strictly by hand, they had no heavy equipment at their disposal.

Just after leaving Cartagena they blew one of their motors. The propulsion engines were LN 2500 Jet engines, the same as on a DC 10. They had four of them and one quit, it blew itself out and you could hear it all over the ship. The engines produced eighty thousand horsepower and operated two screws. They generated thirty plus knots. They had to go to Naples, Italy to a naval base to have the motor replaced. They were there four days.

He said that he wasn't real big on Italy. The people were nice but the area was too dirty and the food left something to be desired. Then they went around to the heel of Italy to Guido and made a port call. He said that was a little bit better than Naples. They spent three days there.

From there they went to Marseille, France, he said that he had been there three times. Then to Toulon once, then to

Saint Raphael, all just port visits along the coast. At Saint Raphael they couldn't pull pier side. The draft was too deep so they had to anchor out a way and they would run liberty boats back and forth so they could get ashore. The seas were kind of rough and they were able to get ashore but they weren't able to get back for about two days. The French Navy put them up at the French Naval Base there. Housed them and fed them until they could get back. Once at Toulon he volunteered to attend a gathering of the Mayor of the town and different dignitaries along with the Officers of his ship. He had to dress up in his dress blues and they had all these French Naval Officers and they put on a meal. He said that he and a couple of others were just brought along for show. He said that the French cuisine looked scary but he found that it was delicious.

He went to Dubrovnik, Yugoslavia and he said that it upset him when the original Yugoslavia got split up because Dubrovnik was a beautiful city. They pulled into Dubrovnik and they would go into town and they heard of a place called Old Town which was an old castle which had a working draw bridge, working moat, clean, no odors and when you went in they had dance halls, shops, eateries and bars. They spent all their time there. When Yugoslavia was broken up Dubrovnik was trashed.

When Greg was asked about communication with all the people in all the countries that he visited, he said that it was difficult sometimes but usually they were able to get the thought across to get where they wanted to go. He said that in Italy it was different. The Italians talked with their hands and they got to where they ignored what they said and just watched their hands and could usually get to where they wanted to go and do what they wanted to do. Amazingly enough a lot of people spoke English.

They next went to Aegean Sea for a while and did some maneuvers. They worked around a part of the Soviet Union fleet. They came out with their latest aircraft carrier, The Kremlin, surrounded by her battle group of cruisers and destroyers. They were in international waters so that they were able to take pictures.

Then he said that they had to cross the 'line of death' in Libya. Across the entrance to the Bay of Khalij Surt, Khadafi had drawn a line that was called the Line of Death that he had threatened to destroy anyone crossing. He said that any time that they got near it they crossed it. Nothing ever happened.

Then they went to Alexandria, Egypt and then took a ride down to visit the Pyramids. Their intention was that they were going to climb to the top of the Pyramids but the Egyptians stopped them. They were informed that if they insisted on climbing the Pyramids that they would be imprisoned so they backed off that idea. They went from Alexandria to Cairo and have been there twice.

He spent Christmas in 1989 in Marseille, France for a week and a half.

He said that he visited Haifa, Israel three times and they would do some exercises with the Israel Navy some times. He said that they had very small boats about the size of our Hydra foils. They were extremely armed with guns and missiles.

On his first cruise his last port was Haifa then straight back to Norfolk, Virginia where the ship went through normal maintenance. They got back in April of 1990 and spent about a month then they went down to the Caribbean.

In the Caribbean they performed what was called a drug enforcement operation along with members of the Coast Guard. They would receive information on different ships they wanted to check out and they would intercept it. Then the Coast Guard would take over. Being a qualified helmsman, he would transport the members of the Coast Guard over to the ship for inspection.

Gregory being a qualified Navigator he navigated the ship at least once or sometimes twice each and every day. He would average six to nine hours on the bridge each day. It's a great responsibility to navigate a billion dollar ship. His initial training was in Orlando, Florida but aboard ship it was a continuous learning experience. There was actually a lot to do and there is what is called a threat area which is a certain area of the world that they would have to be prepared for immediate response. The ship had a draft of thirty six feet and some areas such as the Aegean Sea among the islands there is a lot of shallow water where you could run aground. The Med, the Black Sea and any where along the west coast of Europe and the West coast of Africa was what they considered a threat area. They had to keep their charts up to date. Ships are sinking all the time and effect traveling water ways so you have to keep your charts up to date. A good example of this is Stockholm, Sweden.

That was part of his second Med cruise around seven months. They would stay with the Carrier and he said that when the carrier launched their airplanes they were useless. After a launch his cruiser controlled the airplanes, the Air Officer was aboard his ship because they had the radar system to back them up. The Carrier has radar but not as good as the Cruiser so it was turned over to them until the planes returned and then the Carrier took over to home them in.

During his Naval career he has enjoyed an awful lot of travel. He's been all over Europe and he's been to Guantanamo, Cuba and the Caribbean, San Juan, Puerto Rico, Martinique and at St Thomas for four days, a beautiful place for snorkeling and other water sports. St Thomas had beautiful beaches and amazingly clear waters for snorkeling, Scuba diving and seeing marine life. The waters are warm and like a turquoise clear.

Greg compared these waters with the waters of the Mediterranean that are really cold but also very clear. Rhodes, Greece he exclaimed as an awesome place. It's where the old Colossus was and still is except under the sea. It's another fort
That used to guard the entrance of the waterways to Greece. Beaches were white sand and the town was very clean. It's a large tourist attraction with stores souvenir shops, restaurants and everything to attract tourists. They entered there along with an aircraft carrier, the Forrestal, and when you get that many Navy and Marines going ashore it usually trashes a town. In Rhodes it didn't even make a dent because they had over fifty thousand tourists there at the time. He said that if there was any one place that he would like to go back to it would be Rhodes, Greece. He said that St Thomas and Martinique was the same.

Then his ship went back to Norfolk for repairs, it had cracked a screw.

It was the period when Saddam invaded Kuwait. They didn't go over for Desert Shield but it was debated whether they were going to go or not. They did go over just when the war was coming to a close. Desert Storm ended in 1991 and spent most of their time helping take care of the Kurds. The Kurds were mostly all in the north of Iraq and they were cut off from security and supplies. They spent a lot of time around Cyprus in the Med because the carriers through Turkey would fly a lot of air operations and they would make sure the air was clear so they could fly medical and food supplies to the Kurds. It was called 'Operation to Provide Comfort.' He said that they would also travel in the Red Sea, the Indian Ocean and the Persian Gulf. They would get a threat from Saddam and you wouldn't know what he was going to do. You'd get an alert so you would move into an area and if nothing happened you would come back out. They just helped to protect the Kurds from Iraq. Six and a half months of patrolling the area. They left in the middle of May and got back in the middle of December. They stopped in a lot of ports. They spent a lot of time off Cyprus so the aircraft carriers could cover northern Iraq to protect the Kurds. They also protected transports that dropped off food and supplies for Northern Iraq.

Then they went to Antalya, Turkey, a nice place. they had to anchor out and go in with liberty boats. They had been in the area for fifty days going in circles which is boring and they were looking forward to some shore leave. On the liberty boat they had beer so of course they were all looking forward to some and he said that it was the worst they had ever experienced. They couldn't stomach it at all. The balance of their time there was a lot more enjoyable in a hotel on the beach.

Greg said that one of the times that he was in Marseille, France that he did go skiing in the French Alps. It was the first time that he had ever been on ski's and he about killed himself. He started out on the kiddie hill falling down while just putting on his skis then he even managed to fall off the ski lift several times. After several attempts he did manage to get to the top of the hill and ski down the whole way. Unfortunately it gave him some unfounded confidence and he and a couple of the others decided to go up on the big hill. He went up and put his skis on and looked over the side and thought 'I'm not doing this'. Over he went with a little push on the middle of his back and after a few tumbles he took his skis off and started walking. He said he was falling down every five feet. About half way down it didn't look to bad so he put his skis back on and started skiing again. The sun had come out, it was midday and it was warm so that he was skiing in his t-shirt. The snow was beginning to turn into ice which made him go extremely fast. He was traveling straight down the hill afraid to make any turns and he was flying when he realized that at the bottom he was heading straight at a building. He knew that he had to do something because he didn't know how to stop so he just fell down. Skis, poles and he went flying all over the place but he did stop before he slammed into the building. That was his first and last experience with skiing. He said that he didn't get hurt bad, just a few bruises here and a few scrapes there.

They also went up into the Black Sea because the Soviet Union was no longer the Soviet Union, it was Russia now. They went to Varna, Bulgaria and Constanta, Romania. He said that the towns weren't that great but the people were really nice. He said that they were sitting in a movie house in Romania and Terminator Two just came out, it wasn't really a movie house because it was just a big TV up on the wall. The movie was in French and none of them spoke French with a lady dubbing it into Romania, which they didn't understand either. There was a Romanian Naval Officer sitting beside them that spoke English so he started translating for them. He said that in four days there he didn't even spend ten dollars and he did everything that he wanted to do. The Naval Officer was a lieutenant and he made the equivalent of about fifty dollars a month. He said that there were five of them and they traded in a bunch of money and the Officer showed them around for the next four days. He took them every where and showed them the town and sights. At the end of their stay they had all this money left over so they gave it all to him. He figured it was about five or six hundred dollars of Romanian money. It was almost a years pay for him. He objected to taking that much money but they convinced him that it was no use to them.

He said that in four years he had seen a lot travel in many countries and he wished he had stayed in. It was a great experience and he recommends it to any young person. He said that where else could he get a chance to go to Russia or travel as much of the world that he did. He visited Yugoslavia before it was all split up into several smaller countries with it a much smaller country. When they pulled into Murmansk, Russia the town was kind of run down but the people were great. He said the he traded in twenty five American dollars for twenty five thousand ruples and they were there four days and he enjoyed the best they had to offer in food, souvenirs, drinks and entertainment and at the end he still had ten dollars left. He's visited Sweden, Norway, Germany, Scotland and all of those places.

His second cruise was completed in December or 1991. then after a leave they did what he called work ups – going in and out up and down the coast making sure the equipment is running good. Shake down cruises. Then in May they left for the North Atlantic and the first port they hit was Kiel, Germany off the Baltic sea. To get there they traveled up through the English Channel to the North Sea to Stockholm, Sweden which took you about seven to eight hours to traverse around all the little islands to enter Stockholm. Then to Oslo, Norway which was also a tight fit. They then went around the Norwegian Sea to the Barents Sea and Murmansk, Russia where a lot of the Russian Subs are still. It was a rough course due to a lot of navigation needed around islands, sunken vessels and shallow waters. They spent about eighty seven days up in the North Atlantic and then came back and went into dry dock to have some work done under the ship. Then they just did shake down cruises again up and down the coast to Miami and so on. There was always something different to see.

Then due to the fact that they were preparing for an extended tour they separated him a little early on May 13,1993. He hung around Virginia for the rest of the summer working odd jobs on a couple of fishing boats.

While in the service he went through a short lived marriage. Then after getting out of the service he met his second wife.

He married Tammy Arbogast, February 1, 2000, and is now blessed with three youngsters, One girl and two boys. He said that he would encourage any one of the three to join the military, any branch. But if they decided not to join he said that it was fine to, he wouldn't try to make them.

His decorations and medals consist of Joint Meritorious Unit Award, Southwest Asia Service Medal, National Defense Service Medal, Coast Guard Special Ops Ribbon, Sea Service Deployment Ribbon (2 awards), Good Conduct Award.

His rank upon discharge was Petty Officer 3rd Class (E-4).

He keeps in touch with Rex Parker and wife Keren. Rex served in the Navy in the Submarine service and retired after 20 years. Rex's wife Keren was from his home town and he ran into her in 1989 at a local bar and they now live in Virginia.

ISBN 1-41206138-5